Thoughtforms

~Quanaah Publishing~

Quanaah Publishing

www.quanaah-publishing.com

Thoughtforms

©Copyright 2015
Quanaah Publishing

Written/Edited by S. Quanaah
Cover Design by S. Quanaah

-FOR TRAINING AND PUBLIC SPEAKING INFO-

S. Quanaah
EMAIL: atlantisbuild@gmail.com

www.atlantisschool.blogspot.com
www.youtube.com/quanaah
www.soundcloud.com/atlantisbuild

Printed in
The United States of America

Introduction

The purpose of this book is to share a conceptual-based cultural framework of Knowledge of Self [KOS]. This framework is written to guide those who are on the path of growth and development. "Thoughtforms" encompasses ideas [nonphysical entities] about how societies change and develop, psychological/social behavior, power dynamics, social structure and the science of everything in life from the cultural perspective of a Five Percenter.

-S. Quanaah

A Year in Review

Reflecting upon the past year and looking towards the next Gregorian calendar year, I just wanted to take a moment to share some of my thoughts with all of you... First and foremost, I want to THANK all of you who invest time in reading my articles, researching the links/information I share via my Facebook page, checked out and subscribed to my Youtube channel (A.S.I.A. TV), purchased my literature/music (Quanaah Publishing) and connected with me in whatever capacity we were able to. It is very much appreciated!! The numerous dialogues, testimonials, letters, questions, and constructive advice I receive on the daily lets me know that what I do is not in vain b.u.t. is serving my intended purpose; encouraging positive growth & development. There are also many people I've had the pleasure of meeting for the first time and others I've had the opportunity to build/rebuild relationships from all over the world. None of us are in each others lives by chance, and I look forward to what these bonds continue to positively produce for the future. You are also all very much appreciated!! Last year has been one of the most productive, progressive and positive years I've had. My Queens are doing very well, I'm very happy about our state of health, and there were many things I was able to consistently and successfully accomplish. As far as resolutions are concerned, I don't have any. I am a work in progress so I'm always exploring ways to improve myself so that I can be a greater resource to others. Living a way of life that includes the phrase 'striving for perfection' as a part of its fundamental principles is the essence of any/all resolutions. Therefore, I will continue being as resolute as I have been.

For those of you who've made resolutions this year, here are 9 points I revised from an article I wrote a few years back that will help you achieve your goals in this upcoming year:

* Although it is your personal resolution, your resolution should be something that improves (progresses) you with the intent/consideration of making you a better resource to others and this world we share. Life is interdependent, we all play a role in how the world turns, and there is a constant process of giving and receiving. This intent/consideration ensures that our Resolution is in tune with the universal order, and is something that is sustainable -because we are actively providing a service that others, and the world, needs. If all we are thinking about is what we can get (keep), and not what we are able to consistently give, what we get (keep) will eventually run out. If you don't believe this, try it with your breath. Keep it to yourself and see how long it takes for your oxygen to run out...

* Make sure our wesolution is real and obtainable. It's less likely we're going to change EVERYTHING at once, so it's important to work on what we can change, one goal at a time. Also, take things one day at a time.... It took awhile to create habits and it's going to take time to change them. The smaller goals we accomplish serve as stepping stones; helping us build confidence, and gain the tools & experience that are necessary to achieve our larger goals. And with any goal, one of the first and most important steps we need to take, and habits we need to create is to "Get our day underway with a positive, productive attitude." That attitude sets the stage for our altitude.

* Make your goals specific. Instead of saying something like, "I'm going to read more" say something more specific like, "I am going to read two novels every month." This is called specificity. This not only helps you better focus on your goals, but it encourages you to be more responsible and committed to your goals. If you were to say, "I want to be healthier this year" there is no sense of ambition or plan of action to achieve that goal. Now if you said, "I am going to only eat baked chicken once a week and go to the gym three times a week for 1 ½ hours" that has a sense of ambition and provides part of a plan of action to achieve your goal of being healthier this year. If it's not clear, your path won't be cleared.

* Set a projected time/date for your goals. Setting a time/date creates a sense of urgency, responsibility, and accountability to meet your goals. If you don't meet your time/date then set another one. Without setting a time/date then we're saying our goals aren't really a priority (important) -because under these circumstances they can happen any time, and any day. That is not resolute, and if you don't have a time/date, there will probably never be a time/date.

* Write down your resolutions. I've known people who had challenges with organizing their day, appropriating their time, and focusing on achieving their goals. One of the solutions I shared with them was writing down their goals on index cards or signs and posting them in visible places around their home. This helped reinforce/remind them of their goals so they wouldn't allow themselves to get lost in the hustle & bustle of the day.

* Only share your resolutions with those who have shown themselves to be supportive of you fulfilling them! If they're not there to help you, then they're only going to hinder.

* Look into networking with people/organizations that will help you fulfill your physical and mental health goals. If you want to

cut back on the substances you've been using like drugs/alcohol, or have some mental health issues going on, reach out to any local, regional, national organizations that specifically deal with drug/alcohol abuse and mental health. There are no resolutions when you don't have your health.

* Keep a positive outlook! Some days it will be easy to maintain a level of positivity and other days you need 'social equality' (fellowship) with others -who share the same goals and are just as resolute as you are about positivity. This means, whatever religious, cultural, or secular organization you are a member of or affiliated with, invest the time to be there and learn as much as you can about the positive principles/values they're sharing with you. This is part of your foundational network and will help you maintain a positive outlook when you need the support, which we all do.

* Your resolution is not the end all be all. Some people live to have a wedding while others strive to be married, have a family, and etc... While the former is a place, the later is a state. So although your resolutions may help you arrive at a place, the ultimate goal should be to achieve a state of existence. And this state of existence should set the stage to help us achieve even higher/greater goals! It's all about constant growth and

elevation, not stagnation. Life is constantly changing & evolving, and so should the living.

In closing, I want to wish every one of you and our families a very safe, happy, healthy and productive year! I also will that while reflecting on this past year, we consider those negative things we've held fast to that has not only destroyed our ability to unify with others, b.u.t. has undermined our ability to accomplish anything significant on our own. If we think/know we have offended, wronged or hurt somebody, then take advantage of this moment in time to apologize. If you think/know you've been offended, wronged or hurt by somebody, then take advantage of this moment in time to forgive. Begin your New Year with the right mindset, on the right foot, and making the right decision to move forward. We've all had challenges within ourselves, and with others, this past year, and I will that this year is much more positive and progressive for us all!

How Are We Invested?

Corporate Pyramid Structure

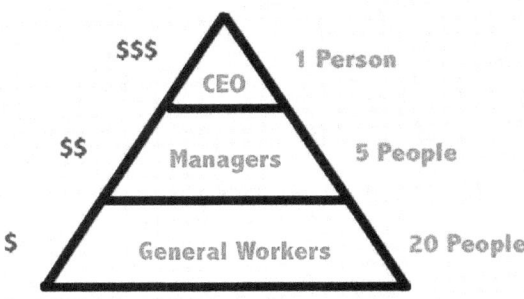

Egalitarianism: A belief in human equality especially with respect to social, political, and economic affairs. A social philosophy advocating the removal of inequalities among people.

Recently I posted a status on my Facebook page about one of Quanaah Publishing's success stories; a brother named Rasheed Carter, an urban novelist. Some time after that it was brought to my attention that some people misinterpreted this success story, the promotion of our company's services, and my brief elaboration on our mission statement -political and socioeconomic equality-, as an attack against others. Although I thought my intention for sharing that perspective was clear, I'm glad that I was made aware that it wasn't, and it would be good to further elaborate on what I meant. These are opportunities we rarely get to clarify something because unless someone is a member of the press, or is orientated in a way to ask questions to understand what someone means, people usually don't ask a person further questions to get clarity on what they meant. They usually just assume what this person meant, and may even go as far as share that perspective with others, without ever taking the initiative to ask the person who actually made the statement, "What did you mean when you said...?" When I ran for public office and put out my official press release on July 4th, 2013, I had to deal with an issue like this. One local publication took the press release, made an interpretation about something I said, didn't reach out to me for clarity, put words in my mouth, and printed it. After reaching out to them to clarify my statement, the publication had to retract their statement [perspective] in the next issue -which said alot about the publication's credibility, and journalistic integrity.

As a writer, musician, cinematographer, or etc., making the transition from creative artist to doing it as an actual business is not always simple, especially in a capitalistic society. Before I began to publish my literature and put out my music, I made sure I did the research to find out what business models served my [our] best interest as a creative artist, and that simultaneously allowed me [us] to maintain my [our] cultural integrity and intellectual property. All of the companies I came in contact with and researched didn't offer this opportunity. It was always a contract agreement where for a certain upfront cost, paid royalty percentage of each unit you sell, acquisition of your creative [copy] rights, and accepted creative direction, a company would be willing to let you work for them by putting out your book, music, or film. If was never an egalitarian arrangement that advocated political and socioeconomic equality between the creative artist and the company. From performing as a poet/emcee since the mid 90's, learning how the music industry worked and negotiating a contract with Razorsharp Records [circa 1997], to publishing articles for various publications [circa 1999] and blogging since 2005, this insight is what ultimately inspired me to found Quanaah Publishing/Quahadi Music. This medium allowed me to self publish my own literature, producing/manufacture my own music, and retaining all of my creative [copy] rights. Next I began to share my knowledge and use my resources to help empower other creative artists to do the same thing; control their own creative destiny by having direct access to publishing and manufacturing their own products.

Author Rasheed Carter and Paul Dyster, Niagara Falls Mayor

I met Rasheed at our local library one day in 2010. He was fresh out from doing a 5 year bid, jobless, and staying in a half-way house down block. He had one outfit and the only property to his name was a black garbage bag full of notebooks; about four novels he had written while he was locked up. We built for a bit, I told him that I knew how he could self-publish his literature, and I assured him that I'd walk him every step of the way. His first book I helped him publish through his own company Profound Publishing is called Young Savage. His second book, Wild for The Night, he only needed some consultation. 2014, and five self-published books later, Rasheed is self reliant, writing more than ever and in a strategic position of putting others on who aspire to do the same thing. His success means my success, and I desired for him what I also wanted for myself. Over time I've used Quanaah Publishing to successfully assist other creative artists in the same way, and I'm very proud to say that as people become more aware of these opportunities to take control of their own creative destiny, we will continue to be at the forefront to assist them. To me this is not simply a noble idea, it's an important investment in a legacy that truly empowers people, teaches cooperative economics, and reinforces the kind of solidarity we need to build strong relationships and communities. In the most simplistic terms, it's the idea of wanting for others what we truly want for ourselves. Unfortunately, in a capitalistic society rooted in competiveness, it's in the best financial interest of some businesses to not provide people with equal access to some opportunities because they'll only breed competitors. In this regard, personal advancement, material acquisitions, and maintaining trade secrets come before the collective advancement of the people.

When I ran for County Legislature in 2013 and participated in a Meet The Candidates Forum, one of the things I mentioned in regards to our voting district is that over 90% of the people who owned businesses here, and secured a living for their families, did not actually live in our district, didn't spend money in our district, and couldn't vote in our district. This, to me, was a fundamental problem when it came to building and sustaining our local economy. It's a problem because the majority of the money these businesses made never circulated within our community; it left at the end of each day and was used to personally advance the business owners, and be reinvested in another district [community]. Because of my personal experience running for public office, and learning the politics of campaign donors and lobbyists, I gained first hand knowledge of where many of these business owners lived; in suburban neighborhoods, oftentimes in mansions, where their children attended schools and participated in activities far removed from the hood that fed them. So going forward, I continued to speak publically and use social media to elaborate on the importance of "localism", encourage people to research and invest in Co-ops [Cooperatives] -one the fastest growing and successful egalitarian business models to build local living economies-, and warn people against patronizing businesses that are not supporting our communities. Obviously everyone didn't like me sharing this, and some quietly ostracized me for encouraging people to critically examine how we, and others, are truly invested.

Oftentimes we hear people speak about how others "keep our people apart from their own social equality", yet the way some of us choose to interact with, and do business with one another, may functionally promote the same idea. Some of us only promote social equality in theory, and are willing to socialize with eachother about equality and fairness. Yet at the end of the conversation, we all go back to the personal household income we came from. When it comes to advocating real socioeconomic equality, and providing fair access to eachother's finances and resources to advance collectively, we don't do it. To truly advance as a group, there are three ways we must be willing and able to consistently interact with eachother:

1.) Give eachother the shirt off of our back who clearly don't have one.

2.) Teach eachother, step by step, how to create shirts for themselves.

3.) Show eachother exactly where they can get/own the same quality shirt we have.

Of course relating with eachother like this, in a way that is fair, transparent, and mutually beneficial, is easier said than done because it requires trust. Yet in order to learn to trust one another, we have to be trustworthy, and demonstrate beyond a shadow of a doubt that we have someone's best interest at heart. Right now, there are still too many of our people just being opportunistic. Instead of building true family alliances, we're making commercial arrangements, and the majority of the time the person making that arrangement lives on a one-way street. If put in the same circumstances of meeting Rasheed, they would simply employ him in order to use his talent to further advance their personal interests, not empower him to be a self-published entreprenuer in order to take control of his own creative destiny. Am I against capitalizing, making a profit, or taking advantage of an opportunity? No. I'm against the notion of capitalizing off of the public, in the interest of privately advancing ourselves. Therefore, the various programs/initiatives I've done and do through my organization A.S.I.A., our Quanaah Publishing/Quahadi Music projects, and my run for Public Office to represent my district all reflect of the same common cause: to inspire, empower, and educate people.

In closing, I would like to say to all of you who're are reading this, who're connected on my social networks, who've read my books, and/or watch my videos, if you would like to know what I meant by anything I've said, please feel free to reach out to me. I'd be more than happy to clarify it for you: atlantisbuild@gmail.com

The Blaque Male Image

In celebration of Woman's History, Blaque Magazine published an article promoting the idea of understanding a wo(man) better which included the above image of black men wearing heels. Blaque Magazine online is an urban lifestyle web magazine geared toward professional women and men in South Africa. Although this cover appeared in the August 2013 eidtion it has resurfaced due to the growing effeminization of the black male climate growing within the Hip Hop and black/brown communities. In February of the same year I wrote an article for Socyberty.com entitled "Hiphop Culture 101; in Defense of Lord Jamar" that articulated the cultural stance of Hip Hop preservationists. Because we now find ourselves addressing the same issue, often with much more fervor, I wanted to take a moment to add-on further to this topic and share some ideas of what we can do about it.

First and foremost it's important to understand the context of the situation. As black and brown people, we are not the major stock holders, institution establishers, media moguls, government authorities, or military force in America. We are disproportionately the minority when it comes to actual power dynamics. We have the potential to be much more with our solidarity, yet collectively we are still not self actualized as a group. There are various pockets of us being progressive in our own way, and some black millionaires sprinkled in here or there, yet as a whole, we are still a very poor, disenfranchised, underclass group of people in America. At the same time, black and brown people are also the most religious and conservative, especially Bible Belt black and brown people. Given this context, much of the outrage amongst black and brown people with the above image and effeminization agenda is two fold: 1.) Many of us know for a fact that we collectively lack the media might to push such an agenda, therefore it's the idea of the major stockholders in America not ours and 2.) As the descendants of

Bible Belt black and brown people who held sacred religious and conservative ideas about the roles of males, females, family, community and sexuality, we still value these mores. It also must be mentioned that chronologically speaking, Europeans and their American descendants have not generally held the same sense of sacredness for religion or conservative ideas as a group. This does not mean that none have, it just means that when you study any of their societies whether it's Greece, Rome, Germany, Britain, America or etc. this high degree of civilization was never the practiced status quo. In fact, these cultures were usually highly hedonistic and provided social mores for a societal underbelly to happily coexist. And culturally speaking, for every one black or brown person you find practicing these customs, you'll find eleven Caligula's that taught them.

Now, given this context, many black and brown people are simply offended seeing and hearing others speak for us, especially on issues that outright conflict with the chronology of our people and our cultural status quo. Additionally, some of us a further offended when we see our own people knowingly or unknowingly parading an agenda or getting paid to promote hedonistic customs that betray our cultural legacy and genetic survival. In terms of homosexuality, this is understandable in a practical sense because another generation of human beings cannot exist without sexual reproduction, which requires a man and a woman. Among other things in considering black and brown people as a group, the concern with the effeminization of the black and brown man and this society's advocacy of homosexuality is this: Can it undermine the reproduction of our future generations? If young males [and females] are not taught about their gender role and sexual distinctions, is it possible they won't be prepared to produce and maintain a family? Regardless what our sexual orientation may be, these are important questions to ask ourselves as human beings seeking to exist.

I recently posted a video entitled "Them" vs "Us" about the growing climate of division within our community that is not the most beneficial posture to take as a group, especially given the context I explained above. History, yes His-Story has shown us that any time a group of people allowed a segment of its own population to be ridiculed, ostracized, persecuted, singled out and demonized by outsiders, destruction soon followed. Why? Because their own people allowed it to happen. Some of our own people feel that what happened to Trayvon Martin, Jordan Davis and countless other young black males at the hands of whites was understandable and justified; they were thugs, wore sagged pants, playing that rap music, and etc. In South Africa, many African Nations sat back and allowed the colonialist whites to persecute and murder the Indigenous blacks because they looked at the ANC as rebel rousers. Even during the time of segregation here in America, not all black people were down with Dr. Martin Luther King Jr. During those protests when the National Guard turned dogs and fire hoses loose on our people, those black people sat at home talking amongst other blacks about that's what them n*ggas get. The same incidents happened amongst the indigenous people or so-called Native Americans when they allowed the white man to take advantage of their tribal disputes, pit one against the other, and have them both sitting on reservations when it was all said and done with. Europeans themselves are not immune. Yes there were undercover Ashkenazi Jews who helped Hitler destroy their own people, and many Irish had to fight some of their own people from starving to death during the Potato Famine in the 1840's. One consistent theme you'll recognize in all of these incidents, and various others I didn't mention, is whenever internal differences exist it exposes a militaristic vulnerability that opportunistic outsiders will take advantage of. A great exercise that will confirm this fact is to research the history of the country where an American Embassy exists. These are the same vulnerabilities being exposed within our community today, as this homosexual vs heterosexual, "Them" vs "Us" environment appears to expand. The reason I mention this is to encourage those of you reading this to take it a step further than just being mindful of the Eurocentric sexual propaganda being promoted through their [American] mainstream media. It's theirs, and they use it the way that they want including speaking for us even if we didn't say anything. Therefore, one of our goals must be to empower ourselves with our own media outlets to use our voice. One of my brother's, Starmel Allah -author of the book The Righteous Way, and various other black and brown people are doing just that. As a sign of pride and solidarity for black manhood, Starmel organized a photo shoot for 300 Men at NYC's Times Square on March 25th. The purpose of this initiative is to provide more images of black masculinity for our youth within our present day Hip Hop community who are being constantly bombarded with confusing sexual messages. Messages such as the mainstream androgynous fashion trends of London's Men's Fashion Week Fall/Winter 2013-2014 collections that are being promoted by prominent black and brown celebrities.

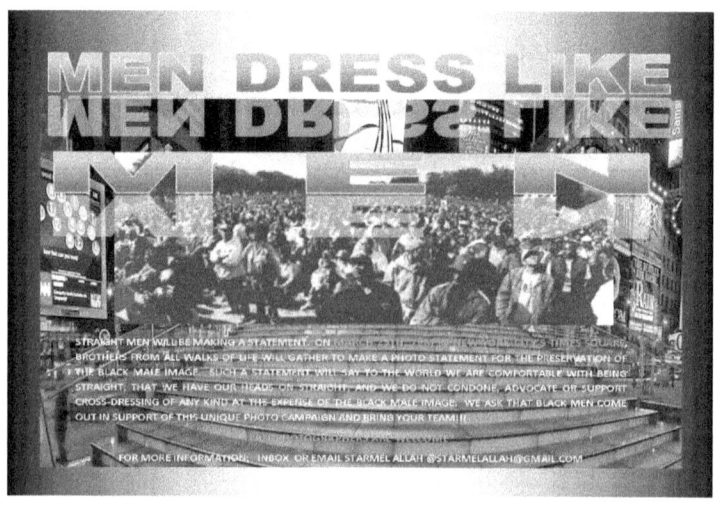

In closing, we also must be mindful of what appears to be, via their mainstream media, growing internal differences within our community where it's becoming an environment of "Them" vs "Us" amongst our own families and communities. These internal differences are not only based upon the mainstream media's propaganda, but it's from the perspective of a mainstream media that has historically kept us a part [segregated], while simultaneously using us to make itself rich from our labor [consumerism]. Many of the things we see and hear throughout the media are being used against us, whether its black homosexuals in a prominent position objectifying and dissing men like the show Fashion Queens, or black heterosexuals making headline news for what was considered an anti-gay slur like when Kobe Bryant was fined $100,000. My view is that our survival as a people depends upon our solidarity, period. As I implied above, like it or not, we genetically need each other for our future generations to exist. All of us, regardless of our sexual orientation, play a significant role in various industries so we also need each other to maintain an existence. We are still family at the end of the day, and don't have to like everything we choose to do, yet we should still not allow our differences to be the reason we neglect one another and allow anything to happen to each other -even if one of us are doing something to put ourselves in jeopardy. We should still care enough and have enough humanity to do what we can to protect each other, even from ourselves. As civilized people, it's our duty to look out for one another, especially when our people aren't willing/able to look out for themselves. We don't have to agree on everything or accept everything we do. All heterosexuals don't agree about or accept everything, nor do all homosexuals. We can agree to disagree. It doesn't serve our best interest as a group, to be so divided, that if thousands of black and brown heterosexuals begin dying off black and brown homosexuals wouldn't care, or if black and brown homosexuals were rounded up and marched into death camps heterosexuals would allow it. We need each other, more than outsiders need our divisiveness.

Open Letter to the NY Post

Good Morning Mr. Buiso,

First I would like to thank you for writing your article "Jay Z is blinging it black", and reaching out to me to lend my "expertise" about my culture -as you stated in your email. It's not often that reporters demonstrate that degree of journalistic integrity by going directly to the source and I (we) appreciate you for taking that initiative. Because we only spoke briefly and didn't have an opportunity to discuss other areas of my culture in-depth, I wanted to take a moment to clarify some things in your article.

One of the commonly held misconceptions is that Mr. Knight, and the group that he comes from, can speak for and define the meaning of our symbols. We are psychologically different in outlook, and cannot speak for each other; Mr. Knight and us, the Nation of Gods and Earths [Five Percenters]. The fact that Jay Z and Carmelo Anthony have chosen to wear our symbol indicates that they want to be affiliated with the positive works they see us do in our communities.

Our movement is more concerned with issues addressing our esteem and self determination than we are at labeling others for their inequities done in American society. Our symbol -the Universal Flag- represents the sun, moon and star: our universal family, man, woman and child, period. And a unified family is the vital building block of any nation of people.

Thank you for your consideration and giving me the opportunity to clarify this. If you have any further questions, please feel free to contact me again.

Peace,
Saladin Allah
Email: atlantisbuild@gmail.com

Occupational Hazards
of the Five Percent

Every job has its own occupational hazards, including the job or the duty of a civilized person. Our 17th degree in the 1-40 asks us "What is the meaning of civilization?" The 18th degree teaches us about our job as a civilized person, which is teaching he [or her] who is savage civilization, righteousness, the knowledge of him [or her] self, the science of everything in life, love, peace and happiness. The 19th and 20th degrees elaborate on the consequences of not following through with our duty, and reiterates our responsibility as civilized people. In these lessons that emphasize our duty, occupational hazards or sources of danger that provoke illness, injury, or the possibility of incurring loss or misfortune are undefined. If we had a thorough Enlightener and a positive support system, they taught/teach us about these pitfalls and how to avoid them. Sometimes this isn't the case and we learn about these pitfalls on our own. These potential illnesses, injuries, losses, and misfortunes are what I consider the occupational hazards of the Five Percent, and today I want to shed light on some of these pitfalls; an effective strategy we can use to avoid them.

Some years ago I met a young man through a woman who stayed in the same apartment building as me. He was in his early twenties, interested in learning knowledge of self, and told me although he didn't knowledge 120, he was holding civilization classes at his house for some of the youth in the neighborhood. He invited me over to add-on and he wasn't lying. When I got there it was about a dozen youth, ranging from ages 10 to 15, in his basement with paper, pencil and a listening ear for what I had to say. This went on for a while and we would hold classes every other Saturday until one day it was like this young man disappeared. Years after that he would resurface and I would see him from time to time in transit. It was always the short build on Today's Mathematics, a commitment to connect, and I wouldn't hear anything from him again until I saw him on the front page of both our local and regional newspapers. According to the press, he was so-called affiliated with a Blood Sect out of NYC running drugs, and the youth he [and indirectly I] were teaching were a team of pre-adolescent/adolescent hustlers being assembled. He was indicted under the Federal Drug Kingpin Law and given 10 years; a charge that carries a mandatory minimum of 20 years in prison, and a maximum penalty of life in prison and a fine of $2,000,000. He was given 10 years due to a plea agreement from cooperating with local and federal law enforcement agents involved in investigating the Bloods and other violent street gangs. Whether any of this was true or fabricated, this is some of what the regional papers printed about his arrest, prior to his incarceration:

"At the time of his arrest, investigators described him as a 'high-ranking member' of the Falls' Bloods set. His home was characterized as a 'Bloods' clubhouse ... used for organized meetings by the Bloods.' Investigators said a large collection of Blood-related photos and paraphernalia was also discovered at his home. 'He would meet regularly with a group of Bloods (at his home),' Falls Police Narcotics Division Capt. said, 'and he seemed to be pretty dominant (in the gang's operation).' The local Bloods set was identified as 'control(ling) a large portion of the crack cocaine and (illegal) firearms distribution in the Falls.' In his plea deal, he admitted to being the leader of a narcotics trafficking street gang for more than three years. He also admitted that he controlled or supervised at least five other drug dealers, engaged in multiple narcotics transactions and earned substantial income from the sale of crack cocaine."

I share this as one example of what I would consider an occupational hazard. To this day I am not sure if the Feds have a dossier on me from simply being in what they defined as a Bloods' clubhouse. With the job I've been performing as a civilized person [a youth advocate within my community/region, online via this blog/videos, publically speaking, publishing books, and operating a A.S.I.A. Prison

Correspondence Project where I communicate with and distribute literature to people incarcerated around the country], imagine the potential losses and misfortunes involved in me getting caught up in a situation like this. Consider the actual losses and misfortunes this young man, a father, suffered from getting caught up in this situation. And when I say losses and misfortunes I'm not just talking about personal losses and misfortunes, I'm talking about positive contributions and support our people, community and society loses from situations like this. That is misfortune. I definitely don't regret the fact that I taught civilization to this young man and the youth in his neighborhood, I have learned to better position myself where and when I teach. And this awareness has allowed me to minimize the risk factors that can result in the possibility of incurring loss or misfortune, for myself, and anyone that I associate with.

Since I've had knowledge of self, there's always been debates about right or wrong amongst the Gods and Earths, and with good reason. It's important to constantly evaluate and re-evaluate the rightness or wrongness about what we say and do as civilized people. I also think it's important for this conversation be framed in such a way that broadens our perspective and our willingness to listen and learn from each other. One approach I've learned is to frame the subject of ethics [right or wrong] as a conversation about occupational hazards (i.e. what are the potential losses of putting yourself and family in that position as opposed to what you [they] stand to gain? What are the pros and cons of that action? How does that choice benefit or hinder your ability to effectively perform your duty?) So instead of just having a philosophical debate on right or wrong, it becomes a practical discussion about effective and ineffective ways to perform our duty as civilized people. In other words, we assess right or wrong within the context of results; "What's in it for you?" as Life Justice would say. If our true intent in being civilized is to mean it, then we've declared that knowledge, wisdom, understanding, culture, refinement and not being a savage in the pursuit of happiness is of special importance to us, and those who mean it too. Sometimes people may lose sight of the fact that we are here to help each other grow and develop. The purpose of framing our builds within the context of results is not only to be scientific, but to emphasize the love and respect we should have for one another, and to maintain peace within our ciphers. We are not URL Battle Rappers and I've been in ciphers where people greeted and departed the Gods/Earths with the word "peace", yet everything they said and did in-between their arrival and departure was everything but peace. Real peace is what links our love for one another and our happiness.

In closing, I want to encourage us to continue working to build and maintain our solidarity by supporting one another in the positive work that we do. Also, remain mindful of the occupational hazards that undermine our ability to stay solid and unified as civilized people. Aside from the external environment of living within this wilderness of North America, jealousy, envy, lust and hate are some of the most significant occupational hazards we're dealing with as a people; they fuel a pursuit of happiness a person hasn't found within themselves. This raises the risk of being a savage and the probability for illness, injury, loss, and misfortune to occur to us, and those who associate with us. Consider all of the risks we've taken, the risks we've seen others take, looking for happiness outside of self. More importantly, jealousy, envy, lust and hate doesn't bring people closer to together, they work to separate people and drive them apart... That's hazardous to any relationship, family or community. Jealousy, envy, lust and hate are the same postures/attitudes 30% of our people had towards each other in Mecca during the time of Yacub. Discontented with themselves and what others were doing, they used their dissatisfaction to slowly draw a line in the sand and disassociate themselves from aligning with their own people. Yacub and his clique of followers then relocated to an island to do their own thing, and the devil was eventually born from this division, isolation, and antisocial behavior.

When it comes to civilization, none of us can do it alone or on an island. Whether we choose to admit it or not, we need each other. The cultural development of our people is multifaceted and requires all of our expertise and participation. The belief that we personally have to be the Leader with all of the answers parallels what's been said about Yacub having a big head, him finishing all of the colleges and universities of his time, and seeking to ultimately possess 366% of knowledge. See, if we are truly dedicated to "peace" and the common cause of performing our duty as civilized people, there should be no problem with building about effective and ineffective ways to perform that duty; we have each other's best interest at heart right? It's not about coming together anymore, it's about being together and doing what is positively needed to remain together for the greater good of the people and our planet. Anything less, would be uncivilized.

What We Teach

Following-up my Open Letter to the NY Post I published in response to the recent media frenzy that cited/quoted me about Jay Z [and Carmelo Anthony] wearing our Universal Flag, more people than usual have been reaching out to me for various reasons ranging from seeking to know more about our culture, to sharing advice with me about dealing with people and the global press. In general, it has been excellent and much appreciated. I spoke on the 5% Nation of Gods and Earths and the Jay Z controversy on Saturday May 31st at 1pm at the MANIFESTO in Toronto, Ontario Canada. Today I wanted to take some time to share with you some of the core values of our culture. The reasoning for this is two-fold:

1.) To elaborate on the idea behind some of the positive works we do in our communities.

2.) To provide an example of a teaching model and general civilization tools for other Gods and Earths to use who are striving to reach people.

The first reason speaks for itself. I think in order for people to come together, regardless of their cultural, religious or secular worldview, it's important to identify a common cause. And one way of identifying a common cause is successfully communicating the idea(s) we share. The second reason addresses something I often see amongst us, Gods and Earths, when we're dealing with the public. I'll add-on about that later.

What are some of the core values of the Five Percenters?

We are pro-righteous and anti-devilishment, regardless of a person's skin color, ethnicity, religion or nationality. If any member of our human family has the willingness to learn to be righteous, we help provide them with the education and tools to do it. This does not mean that they need to become a Five Percenter. This means that if this person needs to be referred to a drug clinic or alcohol detox program, that's where we will refer them. If they need resources for parenting support or academic assistance, that's what we will connect them with. If they're striving to find employment to become more self sufficient, we assist them with that too. The bottom line is this: we utilize what we learn to be better and a positive resource to others. In turn, others can be empowered to assist others. This is all distilled into our simple phrase "Each one, Teach one." Some of us even carry this phrase further by saying "Each one, Teach nine."

The idea that [Father] God and the [Mother] Earth, is the apex of the original [first] man and woman, is a very ancient and indigenous concept corroborated by various anthropologists, archeologists, paleontologists, historians, biologists, and linguists the world over. This means that our cultural worldview, sense of diaspora, and chronology isn't predicated upon, or a visceral reaction to, the short period of two hundred and thirty seven years some of our ancestors were enslaved and segregated here in America. We have recognized our innate divinity, and practiced this as a natural way of life in various societies, around the planet earth, prior to any contact with people who classify themselves as white or Caucasian. Our culture is a unique, contemporary expression, of these classical concepts of divinity. This means that we live our lives according to the adage, "What would God [or the Earth] do in this situation?" Since there is no thing in life, that has withstood the test of time longer than God or the Earth [the creator and creation], they're effective references when it comes to preserving, protecting, and perpetuating life.

We teach and emphasize empowerment through education and freedom, justice and equality for all the human families of the planet earth to live in a world of peace. We view healthy, united families as the vital building block of strong communities, and any nation of people. We also view children as the ambassadors of our future who must be loved, protected, educated and encouraged. Therefore, we do not advocate ignorance, crime, addiction, sexism, racism, poverty, homelessness, hunger, or any thing that undermines our human family's ability to attain and live in peace with each other. As we know throughout history, there are some people whom there is no peace to live amongst, we also acknowledge that their lack of peace must never be because of our iniquity.

While I've only highlighted some of the core values that Five Percenters generally agree on, it's important to understand that all of us grow and develop at our own rate. We are all works in progress and embracing this way of life has given us access to a growth and development process. I am better and more resourceful to others now than I was five years ago, and I'm invested in being even more resourceful to others in the next five years. This doesn't mean that others aren't growing and developing simply because they haven't officially embraced our way of life. Regardless what cultural, religious or secular worldview a person embraces, it's incumbent upon them to find in it what core values will help them become better and more resourceful to others. There were many things I could have gone into, and have gone into in my videos, other articles and books I've published about who and what we teach. Today I wanted to share those things that people can generally understand, and often advocate on some levels, in their own lives. The goal is to learn to better appreciate the positive works we all do in our communities, and recognize the opportunities to work together and address the problems we face, especially our children, regardless to whom or what.

As I mentioned earlier, I also wanted to give other Five Percenters an example of a teaching model and general civilization tools that maximizes our ability to reach people, who want to be reached of course. Why? Because I think many of us are well intended and truly desire to see people become better, and make this world a better place. I also think that those of us who are well intended are always looking for opportunities to elevate what they do for others.

One of the things I've found to be most important for us, regardless of our religious, cultural or secular worldview, is to be better listeners. As a young Five Percenter I would talk [build] for hours. I still can, yet I find it more effective to listen for hours, especially to the people I'm striving to reach. Simply put, how can we do an effective needs assessment of someone if we don't know the ends and outs of who they are, or what they actually need? It reminds me of something my Ole Earth told me as a teenager about not taking girls to the movies to get to know them. She said, "That's two and half hours both of you are sitting there staring at a screen, and learning nothing about each other." As a Five Percenter, with all of this wealth of information we're just waiting to share with people, it's easy to become the talking screen someone is sitting there staring at for hours, and we're learning little to nothing about them or what they need. Some of the information I've once volunteered, and see and hear Five Percenters today volunteer about who and what we are, often creates more confusion than it does an understanding. Take for example someone asking the questions "What is a Five Percenter?" or "Are you in the Nation of Gods and Earths?" Some of us think that it's more important to just answer these questions than it is to find out the reasoning behind these questions being asked before, or if, we chose to even answer them. Imagine the potential or even further confusion we can create in the mind of someone, and whoever they go talk to afterwards, who asks us "Are you a member of The Five Percent?" and we just jump right into talking about Supreme Mathematics, The First 9 Born, Triple Stage Darkness, or etc. This person may have never heard this in their life, let alone how it works, where it comes from, or how it's even spelled! Imagine doing all of that and when the person has a chance to speak they ask, "When is your next concert? -believing that you're a member of the music band The Five Percent. Yes, this situation and various other confusing scenarios are possible, and likely, whenever we don't ask questions and we assume where a person is coming from. So it's very important to first find out what a person knows, doesn't know, listen to them, and then share things with them they can actually relate to. In April when the global press about Jay Z wearing the Universal Flag started to trend, I saw different responses to the controversy by various Five Percenters that would have been a public relations nightmare, had it gone viral. I definitely appreciate the guidance from my benefactors Life Justice and I-Freedom Born for preparing me to address the press when I was approached. I also appreciate others for their positive advice when I was dealing with being bombarded by the global press for further comment, and some of my own people who were not as supportive during this time.

Artist Ramel Jasir

-An ever evolving voice in color-

Anytime we have an opportunity to follow a career path that reaffirms our life's purpose, makes a positive contribution to society, and produces a legacy for our future generations, it is an important story to share with others. I recently sat down with Ramel Jasir, a successful self taught visual artist, to talk about his life's work, family, and how he balances it all during a time when a visual art renaissance is happening throughout the world. This interview is part of Ramel's journey that I've been more than excited to share with all of you. And I will that it inspires, empowers and educates others to pursue their passion, or continue pursuing their passion, in life. Enjoy!

Saladin: Peace Ramel! First I want to thank you for giving me this opportunity to interview you. Although we've recently began to build directly, we've known each other indirectly for many years now, via those who we've taught. I've been checking out some of things you've been doing for some time now and I wanted to expose my readership to works too. To get right into it, let my readers know who you are, where you're from, and a little about what you do?

Ramel: Peace brother and yes indeed we have been in tune with each other indirectly over the years and I must say have been a great admirer of the many things you have been doing over the years in regards to the growth and development of our mighty nation. My righteous name is Ramel Allah Mathematics and as a visual artist I am known as Ramel Jasir. Jasir is actually a combination of two of my son's name. My oldest son's middle name is Jamal and my next to the youngest son's name is Nasir. So I combined the "Ja" and "sir" as tribute to two of my greatest inspirations; my children. I have been an "active" member of the Nation of Gods and Earths since 1988 in which I have spoken at universities, radio stations, churches; organized conferences, founded our annual Family Day in which we will be having our 17th Annual Family Day this August in Victory Allah [Virginia].

In 2007 I was going through a lot of financial issues and the loss of a seed caused me to deal with a lot of anxiety for the first time of in my life. There was an Earth on the west coast who was going through cancer for the 3rd time that recommended painting as a form of therapy and deal with the stress. Needless to say, stress or depression untreated does not get better so decided to follow her suggestions. All I can say is from the beginning I never looked back. Art and creativity became my passion.

Saladin: At what point in your life did you realize that being a creative artist was your path and purpose in life?

Ramel: I think in 2009 is when I decided to focus on taking my art to the next level and actually make a living as an artist after losing a job that I was on for about 10 years. The problems with anxiety was directly related to me losing the job but it was also a pinnacle point in regards to my healing, mentally. I had a lot of money saved up so I was able to go about six months and focus on my craft before going back to work. Within about one year I had developed enough to be offered a gallery exhibition from a very reputable gallery.

Saladin: Some people look at the creative arts as a hobby and something people do on the side, not something as a career. As a creative artist yourself, what has been your biggest challenge when it comes to art being your income producing career? For example, how long does it take to complete one of your art pieces?

Ramel: I think one of the biggest challenges is balancing family life because being a creative artist or what I like to say "creative entrepreneur" is a 24/7 deal in order to really be successful. If you're not represented by a good gallery, you not only have to spend time creating, but you have to spend a lot of time marketing and building your brand as well. You are your brand. You have to spend a lot of time not necessarily finding new collectors, but more importantly, retaining and following up with collectors you already have. As we use to say back in the day "wisdom travels" so if you keep them happy they will show and tell others. Yet this is very time consuming in which you also have to prioritize in regards to family time. Of course the Earth and our seeds want as much time as possible. Luckily, 99% of my work is done at home with my seeds in the same room I create so it is not very hard at times. Yet you can only image what I go through to create with a 2 year old and a 4 year old in the same room.

In regards to how long it takes to make a painting; that varies. Some paintings that may seem some what elaborate and time consuming may have only taken an hour or two. On average though even one of my small paintings can take anywhere from two weeks to three months. It really depends on how detailed it is. I have a solo show coming up in the autumn of this year in Miami in which I have about four large pieces that will take me about two to three months to create. So I will be likely working on them right up to show time possibly.

Saladin: As a writer and musician, one of the things I often consider is family, and how finding a companion who is compatible with our career is important. What advice would you give a creative artist who is considering a companionship, and what are some of things they should look for when it comes to compatibility?

Ramel: Honestly I have to say that it has to be someone who is just as passionate as you about that particular craft or at least supportive. Meaning if you are a sculptor, you may get a lot more understanding and patience from a companion who happens to be a sculptor as well because you share the same passion. You can grow together, collaborate, learn from each other etc. If your companion does not happen to be an artist, it helps if he/she is just as passionate and supportive of your craft as you. Either way you have to find ways to support each other and be involved in the process, whether it is giving you the space and time to create or making calls, marketing, talking up your work and building rapport with potential collectors at exhibition. I think it is like just being a member of the Nation of Gods and Earths [Five Percenters] and having a relationship with a devote Christian or Muslim etc. Some find ways to make it work maybe but it will likely not work in the long run. You don't share the same passion in regards to your said way of life and it will likely clash unless you just find ways to ignore the differences altogether, and focus on the things you have in common, but who wants to do that? For me that is just settling; which does not work. I learned a long time ago that the first time you settle for less, is when you get less than what you settled for in the first place.

Saladin: Checking out some of your pieces, accessories, and etc. you create, I don't get the impression that you're doing "art for art's sake." Everything I've seen appears to have a cultural significance to it, whether it's a certain theme, the people you use, the patterns, or the vibrant colors. How important is culture to your work?

Ramel: This is true, I do not create for "art's sake." I don't create what I think people will like, I create what I have to say about Life. Culture is very important. When I started painting in 2008 I was also learning more about my multi-ethnic background that I was previously unaware of until after my mother passed away and then my older siblings/aunts started to reveal a lot of information about my mother and my real father that no one seemed to feel that I needed to know earlier in life... lol. Everything comes in time and on time I guess so I took a lot of the information in and started to research a lot of things for my self. As I researched more, the story started to spill out onto the canvas like hieroglyphics. My background is very diverse that span several continents and the one thing I found in common regardless of the said race or continent is art. There are cultures/people long gone and languages going extinct everyday, but the artwork and the stories they tell still survive.

I was heavily influenced by aboriginal art when I first started creating which also lead me to Northwest Indian art. My Earth is of Dominican decent so you see a lot of African and Taino symbolism in my work as well. You see Hip Hop, Asian, European, Native American influences and etc. My goal is to introduces people and educate them to the different forms of art and cultures that they may have never learned about had they not came to one of my exhibitions. You see, even though many seem to see the world through the lens of just Black and White, the world is so much more diverse if they would only take the time to see the world community for what it is, not just what they want it to be, or what someone told them it is or should be. One of the must unfortunate things that seems to happen when some get "knowledge of self" is that early on they are given questions and answers yet never question the questions or the answers and recite them with no understanding. That is why Allah gave us Supreme Mathematics and the Supreme Alphabet. He gave us the knowledge and the wisdom so that when we become a "student enrolled" we can approach the lessons from the degree of understanding and not take things on face value; always questioning, always be critical. What understanding is there in knowing the price of everything yet the value of nothing.

Saladin: Indeed Lord. As an active member of the Five Percenters [Nation of Gods and Earths] for over 25 years, I see that you also create various pieces and accessories that bear our symbol, the Universal Flag. Because it has been customary not to just give/sell our flag to any or every one, what method do you use to insure you're not giving/selling your pieces that bear our symbol, to someone who doesn't represent it?

Ramel: I think one thing I do that's different from others that may sell items that bear our Universal Flag is that I do very little to no marketing and it is normally spread word of mouth or photos via social networks. This is usually from Earth to Earth. The closest I may get to marketing is maybe telling an Earth to feel free to share with other Earths. I do it that way because for one they are very time consuming to create and it is for those that are in the know. There are sites out there now that do not ask any questions at all and you can just make a payment and your shirt or earrings are in the mail. Another thing I do is when I see a purchase come through, I send the individual a message advising them that I create the item they purchased only for members of the Nation of Gods and Earths. I let them know respectfully that I only sent them the message because I did not recognize their name or they did not have a righteous name. It would be impossible to keep up with calling every God or Earth that purchases an item to make sure they are on point. There is no way to be 100% sure that a person who may purchase one of my items truly represents our nation. One thing that is for sure, is that the Universal Flag is large and clearly seen and everyone that wears our flag is subject to examination. Our peers are our greatest defense of those wearing something they do not truly represent. Unfortunately, and as we have learned over the years, just because a person can quote 120 lessons or dress a certain way, that does mean for certain that they truly represent our culture. It is up to us to examine all of those that we come across in our travels wearing our flag, even if we have known them for years.

Saladin: In closing, do you have an art shows coming up and where can people go to check out and purchase some of your work?

Ramel: Yes, I current have some of my work on display at the KROMA Gallery in Miami as part of a group show. I am in the process of planning and creating pieces for a solo exhibition that I will be having in the fall at the same gallery so I may do a few small events over the summer but that will be my main focus. You view some of my earring designs at Atabey Hand Creations on Etsy and you can check out some of my paintings. I just started updating that site and should have everything up over the next couple of days. You will be able to see available works and links to my site for available prints. If anyone is interested in commission request for paintings or earring designs feel free to contact me at: rameljasir@gmail.com.

Saladin: Thanks again for taking this time to add-on, I appreciate what you've done and continue to do to make your contribution to this world, and look forward to all of the great things you have planned for our future. Peace Lord!

Ramel: Peace and Thank You as well. I am truly honored and grateful for the opportunity you have given me to share some of my story and creations. Your contributions to this world and this mighty Nation is very inspiring and I look forward to following more of your work in the future. Peace!

Jay Electronica

and

The Freshman Jinx

On Saturday July 12th, 2014 at the annual Brooklyn Hip Hop Festival, all eyes were on rapper Jay Electonica, adorned in a Fruit of Islam [FOI] uniform and flanked with an entourage of Nation of Islam [NOI] believers. After bringing out J. Cole, Talib Kweli and Mac Miller, Jay Electronica finally brought out Jay Z and they performed four songs together before exiting the stage. Since this festival, many have taken to social media to articulate what they believe to be the significance of this event, and today I want to share my perspective on this subject matter.

Heralding Jay Electronica's performance as an iconic return to take his throne, some have declared him as the rightful King of Hip Hop. Others are defining this demonstration with his Muslim entourage as an Islamic Renaissance of rap music; being led by Jay Electronica as a Farrakhan-like figure, reminiscent of the days when the God MC Rakim defined Hip Hop's Golden [Conscious] Era. Jay Electronica himself appears to echo many of these sentiments with the tweets/photos he's posted after the festival.

Whatever those sentiments may or may not be, I think that many people overlook the fact that Jay Electronica is a rapper who has never put out an album before in a music industry he does not control. That in itself is a tremendous amount of pressure and level of expectations that a rapper putting out a sophomore album doesn't even experience. A sophomore jinx is when artists prepares to drop their sophomore album after putting out a classic freshman album. Because their first album was classic, it's often believed that they jinxed themselves from creating a classic sophomore album because the first one was so good. Aside from A Tribe Called Quest, the Wu Tang Clan, and arguably others, there are not many artists who've been able to escape the sophomore jinx. Since Jay Electronica has only successfully recorded some classic verses as a lyricist, he has set a high mainstream bar to put out nothing less than a classic album, classic music production and classic features on his first long awaited album. This is equivalent to a freshman jinx.

You know, the music industry is a very fickle thing, and just as easy as the media loves you, they can hate you the very next day. Ask Chris Brown. So as I'm sitting back watching all of these Jay Electronica fans sharing pictures of him and his entourage on facebook/twitter and philosophizing about how this is a demonstration of Rap's Time and What Must Be Done, I'm wondering if these people realize they need to actually support him, financially. I wondering if they know what soundscan is, what first week albums sales means, if they understand what "merch" is, a HHQ [Hip Hop Quotable] and what a paradigm shift in an industry they don't control will require. Because if not, then all of this social media posturing will be all for not and this critical mass, or 85% of the people I see acting like they support him, will be one of the main reasons for his freshman jinx if it happens. Let me explain why.

Because Jay Electronica has shown himself to be a Muslim affiliated with the NOI under the leadership of Minister Louis Farrakhan, there are many Muslim believers and those whom are affiliated with the NOI, that have expressed their admiration and support of him via sharing pictures, links and comments on social media. Because he is a rap artist, in a music industry, that support is great yet it must be demonstrated in concrete quantifiable terms. In other words, unless this critical mass of people are actually supporting him by buying tickets to his concerts, downloading his album, buying his album in record stores and purchasing his "merch" [merchandise], it would be difficult for Jay Electronica to grow into the cultural arts leader some are declaring him to be. Worst than that, his resources to do more will be limited and you will give the media the means to actually destroy his career. I can see the headlines now: "Iggy Azalea goes Double Platinum, Jay Electronica goes Wood", "Rap's so-called King is Crucified", "Jay Elec-flop-ica's long awaited album is a dud", "Jay Electronica Concert cancelled because of low ticket sales" and etc. Most of my favorite artists are not mainstream, yet in my opinion, they're some of the most lyrical and creative. In many ways, Jay Z publically knighted Jay Electronica into mainstream Hip Hop on July 12th. So the whole idea that "Jay Electronica makes music for the listeners" is no longer the driving force or marketing strategy of his music going forward. It is business and the bottom line is he must now appeal to the masses.

In closing, I want to encourage those of you who are watching this moment in time, and think/feel that it's truly a paradigm shift in rap music, to get involved. Don't just get involved by sharing pictures, links or commenting on statuses. I'm talking about supporting what you think/feel in concrete quantifiable terms. Just because Jay Electronica is giving Minister Farrakhan a shout out and you're feeling good because you're a registered Muslim in the NOI is not enough. Buy a ticket to his concert even if you don't go to rap concerts; gift it to someone who does! For those of you who are 5 Percenters and kith with Jay Electronica, rep his brand by purchasing his merchandise! And those of you who simply like his music, make sure you buy his album when he drops it. If there is any worthwhile demonstration in all of this, then this is what it needs to be demonstration; financially supporting any creative/performing artists whom we truly believe have something of substance and significance they're offering to this world. Chuck D. and other artists have been advocating this for longer than I remember and its importance is still relevant and timely. All of the other empty posturing and "I'm affiliated" politics/pictures mean nothing if we're not invested in artists, or striving to encourage others to invest in them. On a personal level, I am not a fan of Jay Electronica although I do think he is lyrical and I like some of his songs. As an artist myself, artists that have more clarity in terms of their determined idea, a sense of consistency with their body of work and their art itself is what resonates more with me, regardless of the art form or genre I'm critiquing. As I've stated, Jay Electronica is still waiting to release his first album and willfully with his release he evolves to manifest a positive determined idea and body of work that inspires, empowers and educates people.

Controlling the Narrative!

~The role of our Emissary~

The majority of people that are watching what's going on in Ferguson aren't actually there. So I wanted to share what we we're presently doing and what others can do to take advantage of this opportunity to assist and learn from our people who are in Ferguson. Young black males have historically died and continue to die like Mike Brown for no justifiable reason and we need to continue to do what's necessary to stop this.

In addition to the obvious injustice surrounding the cold blooded execution [murder] of Michael Brown by Ferguson police officer Darren Wilson, another concern people have is the media blackout, media bullying by law enforcement and the outright inaccurate reporting on behalf of mainstream media. Because of this, the people have been echoing the importance of "Controlling the Narrative." Well what does that mean? Controlling the narrative is accurately relating and elaborating on a clear sequence of events that occur over time. In regards what's going on in Ferguson, that narrative began when a 17 year old unarmed youth named Micheal Brown was executed [shot six times] by Ferguson police officer Darren Wilson. Outside of accurate 'on the ground' Ferguson sources some of us are connected to directly or are following on social media, the overall narrative has been manipulated and controlled by Fox News, CNN and other mainstream media sources that do not represent the eyes, ears or identity of our people in Ferguson. Historically, this has been a living nightmare for any unrepresented, marginalized, oppressed or disenfranchised group of people living in America and any society where colonialist values serve as its status quo.

Several years ago when I started this website A.S.I.A. I had three faithful readers; me, myself and I. Fast forward to 2014 and I've nurtured a consistent readership of over 100K per month with 60% of July's web traffic being new visitors. That's phenomenal for a niche website that's not selling secrets, streaming porn, razzle dazzling you with products or entertaining you with gossip and paparazzi pictures. As a writer and public speaker, my goal was to do my part in positively controlling the narrative of black, oppressed and poor people in general, and Five Percenters [Gods and Earths] specifically. Before I embarked on this endeavor, I understood that when we're not in a position to accurately relate and elaborate on any sequence of events that occur over time to the world, we're relying on others to do it for us. We've empowering others to write and define our destiny so our narrative, by forfeit, becomes his-story, not even herstory and definitely not ourstory. So from this platform I expanded to establishing a popular Youtube channel/vlog A.S.I.A. TV and took it further by founding Quanaah Publishing; a company I've successfully published and distribute my books through and assist other independent artists with producing, manufacturing and distributing their own literary and audiovisual projects. During that time when I started A.S.I.A. there were various other writers who were an active part of controlling our narrative as well. Today, there are few if any. Today we need them, videographers, creative artists and others, more than ever to be a consistent source of information, empowerment and perspective of this world. If we aren't that worldview, than who will or can be?

NATIONWIDE PROTEST
BLACK OUT MONDAY
SEPTEMBER 8, 2014
WILL NOT PATRONIZE ANY BUSINESS THAT IS NOT BLACK OWNED & OPERATED. THIS MEANS DO NOT SPEND *ANY MONEY* IN PERSON OR ONLINE *

Black Out Monday SEPTEMBER 8, 2014*

WALMART, KMART, BJ'S, SAM'S CLUB, COSTCO, HOMEDEPOT, LOWES BEST BUY, SHELL, BP OR ANY GAS STATIONS & CONVIENIENT STORES, ETC.... *

NO FAST FOOD RESTURANTS OR SIT DOWN RESTUARANTS UNLESS THEY ARE BLACK OWNED AND OPERATED!!!

CONTINUE TO GO TO WORK AND SCHOOL.

JUST DON'T SPEND ANY MONEY....THE BLACK DOLLAR *WILL* MAKE AN IMPACT!!

THERE'S POWER IN NUMBERS!!

IN REMEBERENCE OF

Mike Brown AND ALL KILLED UNJUSTLEY!!

WE WILL HIT THEM WHERE IT HURTS....THIER POCKETS!!

On a local level one of the things we're doing is we created a Ferguson Fundraiser Initiative that's two-fold. First to help fund the travel expenses of one of our community member's trip to Ferguson and to provide financial assistance to any families that are in need of food, clothing or shelter when they get there. Secondly to send our own emissary there on a fact-finding mission to publically document what's actually going on and to connect with local organizers to learn strategic planning that can be shared to prepare our communities here for potential incidents like this. Again, in the interest of controlling our own narrative, if you live in a city/community outside of Ferguson and aren't able to get there to see for yourself and learn what's actually going on, support someone in your city/community who is able to get there. I think it's a worthy investment and makes more sense than just complaining about the propaganda and bias reporting in mainstream media; establish and invest in our own main stream of media by supporting our own emissaries. Even if you're the type of person who isn't interested in actually doing anything yet appreciates a good debate around the water cooler at work, supporting a local Ferguson Fundraiser Initiative is like buying a new reloadable Talib Kweli VIP card. Anytime you get into a discussion with people that have opinions based upon second or third hand information about Mike Brown or Ferguson, you can pull out your VIP card and own the conversation by letting them know you personally helped send someone there and THIS is what's actually going on. Think about it, you're actually putting money where your mouth is and can talk all the sh*t you want for a $5, $10 or even a $50 donation!

In closing, I would encourage those of you who are reading this article to continue to be informed about what's going on in Ferguson and involved in events/initiatives in your area in support of Mike Brown. Continue to put pressure on your local, regional and national public officials to get involved and work to make our communities safer. Sign online petitions and participate in national blackouts to leverage our economic power! Also, here are a few other reputable sources I encourage you to follow and support:

Organization For Black Struggle
Hands Up United
Salim Adofo [NBUF]
Tef Poe
Davey D

Plumb Line: used for finding the depth of water or determining the vertical on an upright surface.

Unity

I recently had a conversation with a brother about naysayers, haters or people who are simply jealous of what you seemingly have and/or who you are. I say "seemingly" because in the grand scheme of things, in a universe that's one where every force and object is interdependent, it's impossible for someone to actually have something you don't. In other words, whatever a person has, whether it's materialistic such as clothes, or immaterial such as patience, it is not a personal possession. Those clothes didn't come out of thin air; they were created from the materials of the planet, with the hands of many people, including those who contributed to its marketing and promotion. Patience isn't an immaterial quality that one person on the planet personally owns. Every one, in some capacity, demonstrates it; some more than others and even a child with ADHD has some degree of patience. Even on a subatomic level we're all composed of the same stuff; undifferentiated matter energy. Psychologically and socially? The source of all thought processes is one Collective Consciousness or Universal Mind. Our brain is a conductor, our bodies are physical vehicles and as sentient beings we interact with one another and our planet. So at the root of any naysayer, hater or person that's jealous of what they believe someone has, is a cosmological glitch. Somewhere along their journey they never evolved to the degree of grasping the oneness of the universe, understanding how interdependence works or recognizing the role of dynamic opposites.

When a child is incarnated [born] and they're discovering themselves and how to attend the world, one of the first lessons they must learn is how to share and cooperate. Developmentally, psychologically and socioeconomically the world revolves around a child for a number of years because its very existence [ex. food, clothing and shelter] depends upon what its parent/guardian must do for them. Every person began from this state of only receiving and giving nothing in return, yet not all people evolve beyond this parochial mindset to understand the importance of equality, reciprocity and the interdependence of our universe. The jealous banter adults make about what someone has or is doing is no different than the teasing five year old children do in a kindergarten classroom. The pouting response a middle schooler gives you when they're asked to clean their room is no different than the antagonism a neighbor shows you when they're encouraged to clean up their community. The petty competitiveness, constant comparisons and insecure commentary 16 year olds make amongst each other in high school hallways across America is no different than the petty competitiveness, constant comparisons and insecure commentary adults make across social media. Some of us have not grown up. Some of us are striving to grow up and some of us could care less about ever becoming a mature adult. As my Enlightener's Enlightener Life Justice once told me, "The child doesn't go willingly, it must be driven out of a person in order for them to evolve."

So what does, "The child doesn't go willingly, it must be driven out of a person in order for them to evolve" actually mean in quantifiable terms? For one, it means that life needs to show a person how to share and that lesson may come in the form of giving away one of your most prized possessions. If we never learned how to work in a group and cooperate, life may teach us the need for cooperation and teamwork with the policies and procedures of our place of employment, or risk being fired. Sometimes people have a toy hording mentality; they're like a child that only plays with other children if they have control of the toys and make up the rules. A person with this mentality often only learns when life puts them in a position where they have no control over all of their toys [material possessions] being taken away from them and they're forced to follow the rules of someone else. This is what I alluded to earlier in this article about recognizing the role of dynamic opposites. Because every child comes into this world polarized, leaning in a way where they depend upon everything for their very existence, part of its evolutionary process is to learn independence and ultimately interdependence. From the beginning, a child is on one side of the scale of interdependence. That side is dependence. The other extreme, or polar opposite is independence. Both perspectives, dependence and independence, are 'horizontally' the same on a vertical scale of interdependence. In mathematical terms, interdependence is the right angle of this horizontal plane. In some circles it's also known as the living perpendicular, being upright or symbolized by a plumb line in the building trades. A person who is heavily dependent and a person who is grossly independent both fail to realize the importance of equality and reciprocity. While the dependent relies on what you give, the independent relies on what they can get. Both of them are primarily concerned about their singular needs and wants, and neither of them have evolved to the point of considering the needs and wants of the collective. Throughout the chronology of humanity, from our most classical endogenous societies to our most contemporary, the greatest examples of peace and harmony have always existed amongst people who demonstrate(d) the highest expression of interdependence amongst each other and our environment. The opposite is also true, the greatest examples of war and disharmony have always existed amongst people who demonstrate(d) the lowest expression of interdependence amongst each other and our environment. This also implies civilization and the degree to which a people are civilized. You can measure the level of knowledge, wisdom, understanding, culture and refinement of a society by how well it provides for and protects its most vulnerable members; its women, children, elders and the disabled. If those provisions and protections are in place, that society will function with a high level of civilization. Whenever you see those provisions and protections not in place, that society falls into a pit of savagery and despair. The story that Yacub was a six year child playing alone when he came up with his epiphany of making a devil when he got older is not a game. This, amongst other things about his upbringing, suggest many things about his maturation process and his personality later in his life. We also learn that central to his life story are the themes of dependence, independence and how this ultimately exposed the importance of freedom, justice, equality, reciprocity and interdependence of the human family.

In closing, I want to remind you that everyone does not mature at the same rate. Some people may chose to never grow up and that's their choice. Sometimes I witness my seventeen year old daughter behaving more maturely than women approaching their forties. Personally speaking, I am far more mature than I was five years ago. With that in mind, it's important to respect where people are and not try to force them to be something they clearly aren't right now. "The child doesn't go willingly, it must be driven out of a person in order for them to evolve" doesn't mean that we go on a crusade to change adults who behave like children. That advice is for our own children and/or children we may work with professionally as educators, counselors and mentors, within the legal guidelines, rules and regulations of our organization and business. When it comes to adults, life itself and the experiences that come along with their behavior is what will change them -if they live to tell about it. Of course we must make knowledge born or share advice with people to save their life, yet when we realize they're not in a place to receive it, we must move out of their way and all of the obstacles they're creating. If naysayers have something negative to say about you, remove yourself from the situation and let your positive works be the consistent response to their criticisms. They project upon you the idea that you think you're more because they actually believe they're less and have less than you. They criticize what you're doing to assist others to try and keep others from critically examining what they're really not doing to assist. They never learned that in a universe that's one, where every force and object is interdependent, it's impossible for someone to have something you don't. In fact, there truly is no "you" and "me" essentially, it's only "we" and "ours" that represents the collective "all." How we reconcile that reality, with our dependent or independent ideas, will define the degree of peace and happiness in our lives. It also sets the cooperative stage to advocate any society of men [women and children] or group for one common cause. The only way we can truly want for our brothers and sisters what we want for ourselves, and genuinely support each other in what we do, we must know and understand that we are one. That degree of unity and sense of cooperation cannot be taught to some of us. Through the growing pains of experience, it must be driven out of us.

A Journey of Sight and Sound

Kontact is my third musical project; a concept album released through my company Quanaah Publishing. Reminiscent of the 1997 film, you are the album's lead character; a scientist listening to coded radio transmissions seeking evidence of Hip Hop's extra-celestial life. You learn that each song contains lyrics of technical drawings that reveal a complex world of advanced civilizations, subterranean folklore and self exploration. Through this sequence of sound sent from a star light years away, you've been chosen to make first contact.

Official Track Listing

Kontact is now available globally and can be ordered through any store that sells music, here at this Amazon Link, my E-Store and my Quanaah Publishing Store.

www.quanaah-publishing.com/our-products/

Brand Ambassadors

In Search of Coretta Scott

Towards the end of the Summer I was having a very in depth conversation with a close female friend of mine. After explaining to her some of the things I deal with as a public figure, and the considerations/challenges that come along with finding a mate, she said something to me that was both hilarious and insightful in terms of compatibility. She said, "Dang, you sound like you're looking for Coretta Scott King."

Her statement made me reflect upon my past relationships in comparison to where I'm at today. In my teenage years the major qualities I looked for in a girl were how attractive, nice and smart she was. Of course this was before I had my first sexual encounters, and when I did.., this also became important to me. Two decades later, I never thought I'd be considering other qualities that are important to me when it comes to compatibility. Qualities that some of my contemporaries often don't understand because there are things I deal with that others don't have to consider. For example, this niche website now receives over 120,000 visitors a month. Although some of these visitors purchase my books/music via the links I provide, this traffic is primarily for the purpose of reading my articles. This translates into emails, messages and inboxes I receive every day from people throughout the world for various reasons; which means a certain portion of my day, every day, is dedicated to following up with people who are reaching out to me. Mind you, this has nothing to do with correspondences I receive in the postage mail or my other social networks Youtube, Twitter, Facebook and even LinkedIn. Add the various initiatives/events I organize or participate in, my STYA youth program I facilitate in my local community, other projects I work on as a creative artist/book publisher and it gives you a partial glimpse of what my world entails. It's a lot, and sometimes feels overwhelming, yet I love what I do!

All of this got me to thinking about how my perspective of relationships has evolved to the point of seeing each other as Brand Ambassadors; someone who is capable of effectively representing your relationship [the brand] at home and abroad [nationally and internationally], in person or via their social media networks. Your brand is your mark, label, identity and what you represent. Therefore, when we're considering potential mates, dating/courting is really a rebranding process and how we're living is a graphic representation of that brand. Fresh off of the campaign trail running for public office in my city, I came upon an online discussion where women were talking about attire to wear at formal events. Some of them, although sweet, were totally inexperienced and didn't understand that flats/sandals or other accessories were inappropriate for such a venue; especially when your companion is the guest of honor where you may be called upon to say a few words. Although this may appear to some as a small thing, in terms of cultural competence, etiquette, social graces and the level of sophistication required to recognize certain social cues and navigate various environments, a woman like this would not be readily compatible for me, brand-wise.

Consider if President Barack Obama had Joseline Hernandez (from Love and Hip Hop Atlanta) as his first lady instead of Michelle Obama as his Brand Ambassador... Sure she may be perfectly compatible with someone else, yet she is not presently compatible with The President of the United States [POTUS] for various reasons. Can she become compatible? Possibly, in time. Yet a POTUS doesn't have time, they have at least four years and that's a lot of public image/relations work and public scrutiny to deal with while striving to fulfill the duties of that Office.

Ironically, Dr. Martin Luther King Jr. chose a woman, who by her own account, was incompatible with him at the time of their marriage. As a young Coretta Scott, she aspired to be in the music industry and had no real interest in MLK or his future as a minister when they met in college. Coretta wasn't smitten, she looked at Martin as short, literally, and in time he grew on her. Even months before their wedding day Coretta was still uncommitted to marrying him and confided these reservations in a letter to her elder sister Edythe. This wasn't a case of cold feet, she understandably didn't want to give up her promising career and become a preacher's wife. So on their June 18th, 1953 wedding day, in which she had the vow "obey your husband" removed from the ceremony and retained her name "Scott", Coretta Scott-King reluctantly sacrificed her dream of becoming a classical singer and became MLK's Brand Ambassador. It was actually in the years following the death of her husband that she was brought to the forefront and became the face, political impetus and momentum to carry on the legacy of the Civil Rights Movement. She wasn't down from day one; she learned to love Martin and his mission. I mention this to illustrate that even Coretta Scott King, as notable and world renown as she is, was unresolved about her commitment to the brand. Today, with the proliferation of professional women asserting their autonomy and pursuing their careers, men are more likely to find women who will face this same dilemma when it comes to compatibility. And many of these women are remaining career women because they're not enountering men with an actual mission.

Keep in mind that everything I'm saying goes both ways! A woman should also consider if a man is capable of representing their brand at home and abroad [nationally and internationally], in person or via their social media networks. Sometimes I see brother's women leisurely post statuses/comments via social media that a woman by my side would get publicly burned at the stake for, but I have to remember, "That's their brand." Some people exist in a world where they only need to consider how their words/actions affect their family members, friends or co-workers because that's the extent of who they deal with and their sphere of influence. In my world I may get an email from France or South Africa about something I say/do or meet some random person who recognizes me in a different state/city who'll ask me about it. It happened, and happens, so I have to consider differently what I say and do. I also have to consider differently how I respond to what people say and do against or in alliance with what I do.

You know, I've been intimate with women over the years, more often than I'd like to admit, yet as I've grown in my purpose I understand the level of responsibility, accountability and scrutiny that has come along with being a public figure.

Even if we aren't, I think being responsible and accountable is important. I also understand that the women by my side will immediately inherit that responsibility, accountability, scrutiny and probably more so because 1.) How society defines females and 2.) The lens females assess each other through. It's a lot to deal with and in some cases I've only shared a part of my world with women in order to not burden them with everything I do. The more I shared, the more they learned they would have to share me with the world, and would ultimately be expected to speak for me in my temporary [schedule conflict/sickness] or definite [death] absence. Some women are simply not prepared to be an active part of a legacy and I've learned to accept that, sometimes reluctantly. The opposite is also true; some men are simply not prepared to be an active part of a legacy and women must learn to accept that. So No, respectfully, I am not looking for a Coretta Scott King. Although she grew to embrace his mission, Coretta was a career woman who wasn't looking for MLK and didn't recognize him, or his purpose, when she saw him. I am looking for someone different.

Veiled Prophets, Profits and Veils

~The Racial Backdrop of Ferguson~

First and foremost I would like to THANK ALL OF YOU who helped support our Ferguson Fundraiser Initiative thus making it possible to send two of our community members Saia HuKeekui and Pocahontus "Cush" Sanchez to Ferguson Missouri on October 10th. Following their return, we held a community information session on October 28th at our public library where they shared their experiences and insights about their journey and some of the ideas we have in terms of organizing locally and continuing to support our community members in [Ferguson] St. Louis. I also want to THANK my Universal Family in Saudi and other community activists in St. Louis who have been a tremendous help to all of us for providing an accurate narrative of the events happening in Ferguson.

WNY Activists Travel To Ferguson

On Friday October 10, Niagara Falls community activists Saia HuKeekui and Pocahontus "Cush" Sanchez traveled to Ferguson Missouri as part of a nationwide Ferguson Fundraiser Initiative coordinated by author, youth mentor and public speaker Saladin Allah.

HuKeekui and Pocahontus.

"We saw that it was necessary to send our own emissaries to Ferguson on a fact finding mission to learn/document what's going on, to work alongside our organizers there and to empower ourselves with the knowledge and experience to bring back home to help implement in our own communities," Saladin said. "This grassroots Initiative is also about controlling the narrative and demonstrating the importance of investing in our own eye witness accounts. Oftentimes people complain about the bias or inaccurate reporting in the mainstream media yet do nothing to address it. This is part of our solution and we are thankful for Warrior Queens like Saia and Cush who are solutionaries."

To learn more about the Ferguson Fundraiser Initiative and/or to donate, go to A.S.I.A. at: www.atlantisschool.blogspot

October 15th edition of the Buffalo Challenger News

One of the common phrases I've continually heard from people living in St. Louis and reiterated by our community members and others who traveled there is, "There's a long history of racism here!" From the 1857 Dred Scott Case declaring that black people had no rights to claiming citizenship, the 1917 Race Riots in East St. Louis and the history of police brutality leading up to the recent murder of Michael Brown, it seemed to make perfect sense until I began to hear about a hidden history, veiled even, that began to provide a clearer socioeconomic backdrop of this divided city.

People with a level of prosperity bankroll politicians to produce policies that protect their profits and property, with the help of the police. In other words, the law is only as strong, and legit, as the people who write it and are willing to enforce it, and these are usually those in a position of power pulling the strings; the elite. In order to understand who is pulling the socioeconomic strings just follow the money. You'll see an elaborate often tangled web weaved with politicians, policies and the police. So in considering [Ferguson] Missouri, let us examine that web.

Approximately 20 years after the Dred Scott decision, a group of Caucasian businessmen got together to found a [secret] organization called The Veiled Prophet Society. Because this special interest group was comprised of strictly members with money/political clout, this was more like a veiled "profit" society. A year before its founding, the city of St. Louis suffered a major blow to its economy due to a strike of its railroad workers, many of whom were black and obviously working class. So the founding of this Society, under the auspices of being civic minded, was really about reestablishing the idea of who was top billin'. And what better way to flaunt this than with a parade? Thus in 1878, this Veiled Prophet Society held its first Veiled Prophet Parade and Fair leading up to what became its annual Veiled Prophet Debutante Ball held in December. Aside from the Mardi Gras-like pomp displayed as prosperity to the public, and racial stereotypes depicted in the floats, what was most notable about this Parade, smack dab in the middle of the post-Reconstruction South, was the regalia and symbols associated with the Veiled Prophet; he wore a white hooded costume carrying a pistol in one hand and a shogun in the other; replicating another Southern-based Organization called the Klu Klux Klan [KKK]. And history teaches us that the Klan's sole purpose was to intimidate, harass and murder blacks and other people of color who sought to do anything for themselves socioeconomically. Their mission, in the words of many white political candidates, was and continues to be to "Take Back America" and the Veiled Prophet Society's Annual Parade -one of the oldest in this country, their Fair and Debutante Ball simply echoed those elitist sentiments. Reinforcing this society's idea of hegemony, prominence and legacy, the Ball culminated with the Veiled Prophet crowning a Queen [of Love and Beauty] from his Court of Honor and given an expensive piece of jewelry to be kept as a family heirloom. In 1972 activists successfully infiltrated the Ball and tore the veil off of the prophet, revealing the identity of Monsanto Executive Tom K. Smith. I think it's also worth mentioning that 11 years later, the Mystic Order of Veiled Prophets of the Enchanted Realm [M.O.V.P.E.R.] or The Grotto [Cave], was founded in the North as an appendant body in Freemasonry. So in terms of special interest groups, there's an obvious link between the ideology and socioeconomic associations of these groups that whites often belonged to simultaneously.

The Veiled Prophet and Gandalf The White (Lord of the Rings)

Fast forward today. This public display of power, with some modifications, has continued to exist as the socioeconomic backdrop of St. Louis, especially in a municipality like Ferguson where only 3 people on its 53 police force are black while the population is almost 70% black. Yeah the Veiled Prophet Parade is now known as the VP Parade and Fair Saint Louis. Yeah people of color can now participate to some degree. Yeah their official throwback flyer looks like a benevolent Gandalf from the Lord of the Rings, but there still remains one common denominator; the same elite controls it. It is this perverse mentality of white supremacy, elitism, exclusivity and privilege that sets the sick backdrop of systemic racism that continues to erode this country and undermine the relationships of the human family, whether it's being carried out through police brutality, redlining, tokenism, crony capitalism or the demonizing and objectification of people of color in their media. This is the backdrop of Ferguson and every other city in America. Regardless how primitive or progressive it appears to be, the power dynamics of race relations are present and wherever you see people of color in proximity to whites, we are not in the seat of power. Even in a chocolate city like Atlanta, whites still control the major financial institutions, traffic system, utility companies, zoning boards, medical facilities and of course the food/textile industry. This article is not to imply that the Veiled Prophet Society is some new age Illuminati that put a hit out on

Mike Brown. What I am saying is that in the eyes of the elite, the lives of outsiders have little to no value. It is only until we look behind the veil and realize that we, people of color and poor whites, have been and are being kept apart from their own socioeconomic equality, can we organize to transform our collective condition. There's a longstanding history, yes his-story, of racism in St. Louis. The kind of racism that helped shape and mold the cultural consciousness of people such as Dick Gregory, Maya Angelou, Miles Davis, Redd Foxx, Donny Hathaway, Maxine Waters, Nato Caliph, Ali of the St. Lunatics [Power God Allah] and Tef Poe to name a few. The events in Ferguson are successfully removing the veil. Not just in St. Louis but throughout this country -and the injustice there is a threat to justice everywhere. Be studious to learn what's going on, assist our organizers in Ferguson financially, with consumables or etc., organize locally to establish a network of support in order to help prepare each other for incidences happening like this where you live. And above all, keep in mind that our "Unity" is the key and answer to solving social ills like this. Whether it's unifying to police our own communities, unifying to support our own businesses, unifying to privatize our own schools or just being a unified voice in rearing our children. It is through this unity can we forge our own special interest groups and ultimately rival the power and shift the dynamics of the elite.

Of course 'All Lives Matter'

According to US Census data, females outnumber males throughout the United States between 50 percent and 56 percent. Niagara and Erie counties are both 51 percent female. Have you ever wondered how females are defined as a minority even though they're actually the majority of our population?

Demographically, it doesn't make sense. Maybe issues concerning females are a minor concern of the dominant society. Maybe it's because females don't share the power, opportunities, rights and privileges as their male counterparts. Here's some facts to consider:

• Even though females are out-graduating males in college they're still under-earning males in almost every degree.

• Females earn about 75 cents on the dollar compared to males.

• Unlike many countries, the U.S. still doesn't have a national law to guarantee paid maternal leave for females.

• Females make up only 4 percent of the CEOs of the S and P 500 companies.

• There has never been a female vice president or president of the U.S.

Because of this historical and present day reality affecting our female population, there have always been people, organizations and movements dedicated towards establishing human/civil rights and fair economic opportunities for women. The facts I've shared, and other statistics, show a historical sexist and misogynistic sentiment that has pervaded American society since its 1776 conception. Females lives matter and we cannot diminish, minimize or trivialize this. That would be equivalent to going to a woman's rally against domestic violence and arguing that they need to stop talking about this because "All Lives Matter" and men are DV victims too. Some may even advocate that dogs lives matter because x amount die every year protecting their owners from home invasions.

Whatever a person's reasoning is for hijacking an important narrative like this, and redirecting attention away from the main concern that female's lives matter, it's one of the main reasons institutional sexism persists. The same lack of consideration and engagement also applies to the infamous "R-word" — Racism.

On Dec. 13, in conjunction with an International Day of Resistance, there was a rally held at Legend's Park to bring awareness to the disproportionate instances of police brutality toward African-American citizens. The rallying cry was, and is, "Black Lives Matter." According to data from 1999-2012 from the Center on Juvenile and Criminal Justice on police brutality:

• A black person is killed extra-judicially (unlawfully) every 28 hours by law enforcement.

• Black men between ages 19 and 25 are the group most at risk to be shot by police.

• Black youth are 4.5 times more likely to be killed by police than any other age or racial group in America.

• Black people comprise 26 percent of police shootings we only makeup 13 percent of the U.S. population.

Like females, and various segments of our population deemed "minorities," African-Americans are also disproportionately affected by socioeconomic conditions including police brutality. Although some of you would love to believe these issue are because black people are on welfare, criminals by nature and/or uneducated, many times we are discriminated against simply because of the color of our skin — the same way many females are discriminated against because of their gender. This also gives you some insight into the degree of scrutiny, bullying and outright attacks black women, double minorities, have historically received when they play prominent roles or hold executive positions within this society. Of course "All Lives Matter," including females and black lives.

In this critical day and time it's important to understand that in the U.S. there are still marginalized segments of our society, deemed minorities that are outright disrespected and discriminated against simply because they're female, they're black or both. These problems specifically affects these groups, not all people, and it must be discussed and resolved because whatever is allowed to happen to the least of us eventually affects us all. We share neighborhoods. We are your co-workers, doctors, public officials and prepare your food at restaurants. We are your children and grandchildren's peers. We are your family members through marriage or birth.

Learn more about the plight of your fellow citizens and what you can do to be a positive agent of change. Knowledge empowers you to "know" the "ledge" or limitation of certain ideas that no longer reflect our changing societal landscape.

Photograph: Dan Cappellazzo [Niagara Gazette]

Black Lives Matter

The following article by Philip Gambini appeared in the Niagara Gazette highlighting a December 13th Rally I organized on the National Day of Resistance against police brutality:

"Legends Park gathering in support of national protests focuses on community issues"

By Philip Gambini

Community members and city leaders gathered in Legend's Park Saturday in solidarity with national protests speaking out against police violence in America.

The gathering, organized by local activist Saladin Allah, was attended by a dozen residents young and old, including Councilwoman Kristen Grandinetti and Council Chairman Charles Walker. In the formidable cold, it became less a rally and more a forum on the issues facing members of the Niagara Falls community and across the nation.

"We are showing publicly that we take responsibility of ourselves," Allah said. "We are not relying on somebody to speak for us and we are not relying on somebody to take care of us."

The group stood in a circle in Legend's Park, discussing a range of topics from the historical treatment of African-Americans, to the family's importance in a productive community, to the responsibility of individuals to learn for themselves about this country's heritage and history.

"It's important that we are mindful and aware of what we need to do for ourselves," Allah said.Resident Ezra Scott braved the December air to show his support. He spoke about critiques of the national protest, whether they were to identify police brutality or community violence. In the end, he said, it is not localized to a specific issue. Rather, it is a gesture of strength to identify that community members who are not often heard have a voice. "Whether it was because of an unfortunate event," he said, "we need to take charge, take initiative, keep it moving, and people are going to follow."

A focus of the forum was that it was not organized specifically around faith, color or denomination. Those present talked of a common humanity that must be elevated and honored if we are to live in a truly equal, just society. The group took time to congratulate the presence of the council members and thanked them for standing in unity with their cause.

"The power behind it," Grandinetti said, "is once you take the risk and use your voice one time it becomes easier and easier ... It's not about being angry or violent, it's about having a voice." She discussed her involvement in women's and children's rights. She asked for those present to raise their issues with positive energy in city government. "We live in one of the most beautiful places in the world and this city should be thriving," she said. "But it's because there's a small group of people who want to be big fish in a dirty little pond. They are keeping it down."

The group also touched on an understanding of historical context. Allah spoke of immigrant community members who had changed their name to conceal themselves from persecution, while Grandinetti recounted her father's own efforts to do the same. "Out of the 238 years we have been in this country, 189 of those years we were not allowed to participate in American society. Eighty-nine years we were slaves, another 100 years we were segregated," Allah said. "That's over 75 percent of the time we have been in this country we've been looked at as less than, as thugs, as savages." Walker spoke how American civil discourse had devolved, rather than progressed, with election of President Barack H. Obama. He recounted his shock at how this president had been spoken about in media, while other members of the crowd noted that his very citizenship had been questioned from the start.

"Our voices are the importance," he said. "We are not going to take this. Collectively speaking out is the only way we're going to change things." Unfortunate as the circumstances in Ferguson and New York are, he said, they have to happen in order to gather peoples' attention and focus their efforts on change. Though the numbers in Niagara Falls paled in comparison to the protests in Washington D.C. and New York City, many of those present dismissed the consideration outright. Any turn out, they said is a valued and important show of support. "In the Bible it says faith without work is dead, and obviously we are a people of faith," Allah said. "But we need some work, straight up work, to go along with that faith. That's what we are, we represent that work."

American Horror Story: Asylum

Allah and Azreal

In May of 1965 after being arrested with several other men for unlawful assembly and disorderly conduct at a rally in front of the Hotel Theresa in Mecca [Harlem, NY], Allah [the Father] was arraigned in criminal court before Judge Francis X. O'Brien and held on a $9,500 bond. Four months later he was shipped off to the Psychiatric Unit at Bellevue Hospital. Allah would remain there until a final psychiatric report submitted to Judge O'Brien stated that "he did not understand the charges against him" thus remanding him to the NYS Department of Mental Hygiene for indefinite confinement. At the age of 37, Allah was confined in these institutions, Bellevue and Matteawan State Hosptial, for two years. Matteawan was a limbo for sadists; a living nightmare used to house people considered too dangerous for civilian institutions yet too ill for prison. It was during Allah's stay in Mattewan that he met and befriended a young 17 year old Caucasian transfer from Elmira State Penitentary named John Kennedy. Because Allah didn't represent a religious group he didn't have the constitutional protection of religious freedom in a court of law. There were always others who considered themselves a diety, yet because they claimed it within a religious context, they were afforded religious protection under the law. Allah was not afforded that protection and some Five Percenters are still being catagorized as 'criminally insane' and denied the right to practice our culture in correctional facilities around the country. Allah also wasn't politically affiliated, a member of any organizations or representing any institutions. Therefore, he didn't have their support, publically or privately. He stood alone, and as he came to learn, the 17 year old Caucasian boy he met in Matteawan stood out, and alone, in his own way too.

Allah and Azreal

Born on September 28th, 1948, 17 year old John Kennedy was Allah's first Caucasian student. As the first Caucasian Five Percenter, John adopted the name 'Azreal' becoming a prototypical model of how Caucasians were educated and entrusted to function within the context of our growing national body. As a civilized man who was empowered with the knowledge of his people, and ours, Azreal grew to educate people on how to survive and avoid the snares of this devilish society, especially mental health institutions. He had a lot to tell because he had been through hell. An institutional hell that he knew so well that Allah symbolically gave him the keys to it.

I knew Azreal personally and one of the things he always talked about is how he suffered in various facilities, especially Matteawan, because of his name. Some of us took that for granted and never looked further into what Azreal may have been striving to communicate. "Yes the President's name was John F. Kennedy and Azreal's birth name was John Kennedy" some of us thought, believing that Azreal was just proud to have an honorable name that many of our people looked at honorably. Well what politics and policies did President John F. Kennedy represent that the guards at Matteawan felt the need to persecute Azreal, AKA John Kennedy, for? Why the transference?

President John F. Kennedy

Doing further research I learned that John F. Kennedy spent his entire political career, as a Senator and as the President, striving to reform the mental health system. It personally hit close to home; his elder sister Rosemary was 23 when she had a lobotomy [brain surgery] that incapacitated her and eventually led to her death. In 1955, then Senator Kennedy sponsored the Mental Health Study Act to begin reevaluating the practices/procedures employed in mental health institutions around the country. As the President of the United States in 1963, President Kennedy authorized the Joint Commission on Mental Health to investigate mentally ill related problems and sponsored the Community Mental Health Centers Act to reform the entire mental health system. This final Act, was one month before his assassination. Following his death, in 1968 John F. Kennedy's sister Eunice Kennedy Striver, partially inspired by their sister Rosemary, started the Special Olympics.

Matteawan State Hospital

I mentioned an American Horror Story in regards to the mental health system because that's exactly what these institutions were, and Matteawan was considered the worst. Along with medical care that was below hospital standards, the institution's practices were barbaric; performing lobotomies and using shock/water therapy, hypnosis, sleep deprivation, starvation and other Spanish Inquisition-like procedures on people as young as their early teens. It's also worth noting that lobotomies were not carried out by professional surgeons nor were they performed in surgical laboratories. They were done in un-sanitized environments with poor lighting, poor staffing and crude instruments. This is not even mentioning the knuckle-therapy, sexual and verbal abuse people had to deal with or died dealing with while confined in these institutions where prison guards were also trained. It wasn't until the 1960's with the political pressure of President Kennedy, and during the time Allah and Azreal were in Matteawan, did the mental health system begin popularizing the use of psychotropic drugs for psychiatric treatment. However, this did not spell relief for these inhabitants of hell; the drug experimentation, overdoses and Thorazine straight jackets made it that much easier to carry out the knuckle-therapy, sexual and verbal abuse.

No I am not saying or implying that Allah and Azreal were sexually abused. Because of the nature of the environment, both of them were verbally abused and Azreal talked extensively about the physical abuse he suffered. Allah, Azreal and others witnessed many of these things and lived to tell about it. Many who survived this hell still carry a mental diagnosis along with physical scars. All of them suffered some degree of post traumatic stress, including Allah. Allah was confined there for two of the five years he and his companions organized the Five

Percenters; that's 40% of the time he was here among us. Have you ever asked yourself why there's not much conversation about that time, or have you even considered how he was psychologically affected? As Five Percenters, some of us romanticize the idea that the Father showed and proved who he was and just walked out of Matteawan unaffected. Just researching the state of the mental health system in this country at the time Judge O'Brien deliberately remanded him to it would show you this idea is unrealistic. The state of this country's mental health industry was so horrific that John F. Kennedy, as a Senator and as the President, made its reformation a key talking point of his entire political career. One of his final talking points prior to his assassination. Given this history, it is my perspective that Azreal was more than a prototypical model of a Caucasian Five Percenter. He symbolized, in the name of John Kennedy, the reformation of the devil's mental health institution. With President Kennedy's Community Mental Health Centers Act he sought to de-institutionalize mental hospitals with community mental health services. This translated into the closing of long stay mental health institutions because of its reduced population, staff losing jobs and companies aligned with these institutions losing contracts [money]. President Kennedy was messing with a lot of people's money, which over time cut 90% of the beds at state mental institutions. Staff at Matteawan were forced to change and find a new hustle. They didn't like that, nor did they like Azreal's honorable name that represented that change. And because many couldn't reach President John F. Kennedy the President to show their dissatisfaction with these changes, they persecuted the John Kennedy they could reach. Azreal mentioned his honorable name, President Kennedy, the mental health industry and his experience in Matteawan often. He also talked a lot about Allah's compassion and insight to not only recognize what we was going through, but to educate him on how to become better. These correlations help us better understand the context of our plight as a Nation of Gods and Earths [Five Percenters].

After standing trial, Allah was eventually released from Matteawan in April of 1967. Some time after that Azreal was also released and came to Mecca to find him. Because of the national political pressure to change the psychiatric landscape of state mental institutions and the mental health industry as a whole, they, and others being held unreasonably, were able to go home. It wasn't because Allah debated a board of psychiatrists about the science of everything in life and they were so mezmerized by his wisdom that they just had to let him go. Nor did Azreal burst out of Matteawan like Chief in One Flew Over the Cockoo's Nest. Allah, like Azreal and others, didn't demonstrate the kind of maladaptive behavior, dependency or learned helplessness institutional staff documented to justify keeping them there. This was the climate of America during this time and slavery by another name; a 'citizen-to-asylum pipeline' that shuffled people into a system they often didn't survive.

In closing, keep in mind that nothing happens in a vacuum. Everything is not as explicit as we may like for it to be. Some things are implied, if we listen, and give us deeper insight and a better appreciation for what others may not say. Azreal and Allah found themselves caught up in a kind of system that many of us could only imagine. They, like many others, didn't walk out unscathed and there were things they saw and experienced that they probably took to their graves. So behind some of the things Azreal said, what Allah instructed some of us to do, and how they coped, is a story. A story that gives context to AWM.

Labors of 'localism' can lead Falls back

I think all of our children need to learn the word "localism" and by the time they reach middle school it shouldn't be an unfamiliar word in their vocabulary. Localism is the idea of prioritizing the local.

For us, it's a "Niagara Fallsian" philosophy of investing in our local businesses, advocating a local control of government and promoting our local history, culture and identity. It's the posture and attitude that we need to support each other. Whether it's supporting our staple businesses like Richardson's Fast Food Deli on Highland Avenue or Steve's Automotive on Main Street, there is a pride of ownership and personal service local businesses offer that is rarely seen from BIG business. Why? Because local businesses like Richardson's and Steve's are people we see every day and there is a different sense of community and accountability in providing products and services to the people you see every day.

When it comes to problem solving, BIG businesses are more likely to route you through a labyrinth of representatives who tell you, "There's nothing we can do about it" as opposed to local businesses who ask you, "What can we do to resolve this?" I don't mind trying to contact a corporate headquarters in a different state or country, but I'd rather just talk to the owner face to face.

I recently had an opportunity to visit two new local businesses in the Pine Avenue City Market — Maple's Restaurant that offers a southern-style menu and a Sunday's Best buffet and The 755 Restaurant and Lounge that specializes in authentic Lebanese and Italian-American cuisine. I actually discovered one, sitting inside of the other. While out to lunch at Maple's Restaurant with local author/business owner D. Scott, we met Hana; the daughter of The 755 owner who was also there purchasing lunch. This was localism at its best; maximizing the circulation of each dollar before it leaves our community. Since then I've patronized both establishments and in addition to the excellent food, I'm glad I no longer need to drive out of our city to get it.

Over the last five years with well over a dozen businesses closing in the city of Niagara Falls, many wonder how we can increase sustainable business development here. While local support is vital, one component of localism is the creation of 'cooperatives' [coop] or 'co-operatives' [co-op]. Co-ops are businesses that are owned and managed by the people who use its services [a consumer cooperative], the people who work there [a worker cooperative] or by the people who live there [a housing cooperative]. It's the idea of shared ownership, work and financial responsibility of that business and co-ops are one of the fast growing successful business models reshaping local living economies today.

Barbershops and hair salons have been running informal co-ops for years. Family owned Italian restaurants, Chinese variety shops and Arab corner stores have been operating like co-ops too. Gui's Lumber & Home Center, which has remained in business all of these years, is a co-op. Living in a state with some of the highest taxes in the country and a city/county with a tax-exempt casino and BIG businesses that local business owners must compete with, this has created a unique set of socioeconomic challenges.

Our city of Niagara Falls can be one of the premier local living economies in the state with the right community support and people in leadership positions that have the shared vision, plan and work ethic to meet those challenges. This is not just a noble idea. It's a commitment to empowering each other with the cooperative economics to thrive.

If not us, who? If us, when?

That Priceless Look of Poverty

"Who Are the 10%?"

Regardless how well intended and proficient doctors may be, they are in the sick business. If they healed patients we would rarely need doctors so they "treat" them instead -and the pharmaceutical companies aren't mad about it. The same can be said about lawyers; they are in the crime, personal injury and family dysfunction business. If it weren't for drugs, violence, accidents, divorces and etc., we would rarely need them too. I'm sure my barber is glad indestructible haircuts don't exist yet because he would be out of business too. Whether we are mechanics, school teachers, dentists, politicians, pastors or etc., there's a certain degree of job security that comes along with fixing things or even striving to insure that things remain broke, as in "poor."

Here in New York, according to the 2014-2017 Community Health Assessment Niagara County Department of Health released in 2013, "23% of the people in our live below the poverty line and 44% of the population—almost one in two—is either in poverty or struggling financially and at risk." In the city of Niagara Falls, approximately 60% of our residents receive public assistance such as food stamps, welfare, unemployment insurance and Medicaid. According to 2009 data, 67% of the families in poverty are female headed households with no husband present, and 70% who are poor are unemployed. Another important statistic is that foreign-born residents are 94% above the poverty line.

When it comes to statistics, people can manipulate them to serve whatever political agenda they want. For example, in regards to 67% of the families in poverty being female headed households with no husband present, some people may simply say it's because they're not marriage material. Some people believe that the 70% who are poor, unemployed, are just lazy. The 94% foreign-born residents who are above the poverty line? Some may say they all work harder. Whatever statistics say there's always an angle of what can be said, which is oftentimes inaccurate or disingenuous.

One of the misconceptions people in my area tend to have about welfare [public assistance] is that their taxes pay for it. In part, they do. All of us who work allocate a certain portion of our taxes towards supporting our public assistance program. The reality is my county receives financial support from [New York] state and the federal government to fund our public assistance program. Because of the statistics related to poverty, and accompanying socioeconomic factors such as teenage pregnancy, poor education and etc., my city [Niagara Falls] receives a larger portion of that state and federal support. In other words, if the city were a person named Nia G. Falls, they would be living below the poverty line, receiving public assistance and parenting thousands of children.

Another misconception is that the face of welfare is "Lazy La'Shaniqua" who has 7 children by four baby daddies living in public housing. Actually, the largest portion of state and federal support any impoverished county and city receives for public assistance goes towards contracts, personnel, employee benefits and administrative services, not a welfare check. So the real face of welfare or those benefiting most from our city's poverty have more common names than La'Shaniqua. They are

114

most likely home owners with a two income household that don't live in inner city zip codes. Do you get that picture?

Now you're probably wondering who we can blame for this. Well I'm not in the blame game business. We need more hands working, less finger pointing and the sober realization that fixing the things that are broke about our cities requires a multifaceted approach; collective work and responsibility. In the process, we also can't be naive to believe that there aren't people invested in things remaining broke [poor]. There are people like that, and they don't look like the broken.

Like with any family going through a financial hardship, we are not alone. On the other side of Canada lives Nia G. Falls' poor cousin Dee Troit -who has also fallen on tough financial times. Maybe we, and cities like us, need to consider what strategies Dee is using to change their financial situation. That insight, may be priceless.

Atlantis Build Talk Radio

Introducing Atlantis Build Talk Radio; the premier station for Five Percenter [Nation of Gods and Earths] Talk Radio. This station is a unique blend of uncensored informed commentary, music and interviews about the science of everything in life.

Atlantis Build Talk Radio is a subsidiary of the A.S.I.A. cultural institution network which has an audience in over 100 countries via A.S.I.A. and A.S.I.A. TV.

This station appeals to a dedicated global audience who want to be "in the know" by delving deeper into subject matters, music and interviews that inspire, empower and educate.

LISTEN/DOWNLOAD Episodes at:

www.soundcloud.com/atlantisbuild

Rest In Peace

Have you ever considered that Confederate Flag waving may be more of a symbol of reconciliation than succession? Or that many southerners, and their northern kinfolk, still feel perpetually slighted by the United States Government? Well consider the fact that in the 1860's, after the Civil War, Congress enacted legislation that authorized the President to purchase "cemetery grounds" to be used as national cemeteries for soldiers who died in the service of the country. By "soldiers" it meant Union soldiers, not Confederate soldiers. Confederate soldiers could not be buried in national cemeteries, nor were they afforded any benefits from the United States Government. So those aren't Confederate soldier names engraved on Veteran's Memorials or Confederate soldiers being memorialized on Veteran's Day -a National Holiday. When the remains of Confederate soldiers were found on the battlefield lying near those of Union soldiers, the Union soldiers were removed, buried with honor and they'd leave the Confederates' bodies rotting in field. It was only because of the fear of disease spreading were their bodies put in temporary shallow graves and marked with wooden headboards for identification. And it wasn't until private women organizations, such as the Wake County Ladies Memorial Association in North Carolina, assumed the initial financial responsibility to remove these Confederates' and bury them in southern cemeteries. Keep in mind that because the Federal Government administrated this construction of these National Cemeteries, former Confederate States also paid for this. Between 1898 and 1968, the government added sections to the national cemetery to accommodate the graves of veterans from the Spanish-American War, World Wars I and II, the Korean War, and the Vietnam War. The cemetery's annex is located due north of the historic original 17-acre property. Today, more than 6,000 veterans lay at rest in the national cemetery and there are almost 4 million people, "non-Confederate" Veterans of every war and conflict, buried with honor in 147 national cemeteries on about 20,000 acres of land.

So here it is, after the Civil War ended, the United States Government buried and memorialized their own, symbolically spit on the unmarked graves of their southern kinfolk, and then made them financially responsible for a large part of constructing national cemeteries they could not be buried in. And to add further insult to injury, black veterans earned a place in the ground and name on these same memorial monuments. Some present day American patriots would simply say, "That's what rebels get!" Yeah, well do you really think that's fair and what about the noble idea of being charitable to the opposition? It's not like every Confederate soldier was a slaver and genetically unrelated to anyone up north; the Civil War was like the Hatfields and McCoy's. The McCoy's won and made the Hatfields pay for a large part of the clean-up, an elaborate cemetery and monuments for the McCoy veterans for generations. Rescue me if I'm wrong but that doesn't seem like the best way to heal open wounds and every year during Memorial Day, Veteran's Day and etc. this history is indirectly, or maybe directly, thrown in people's faces. But hey, what do I know -my name is "Saladin" and I know nothing about conflict resolution.

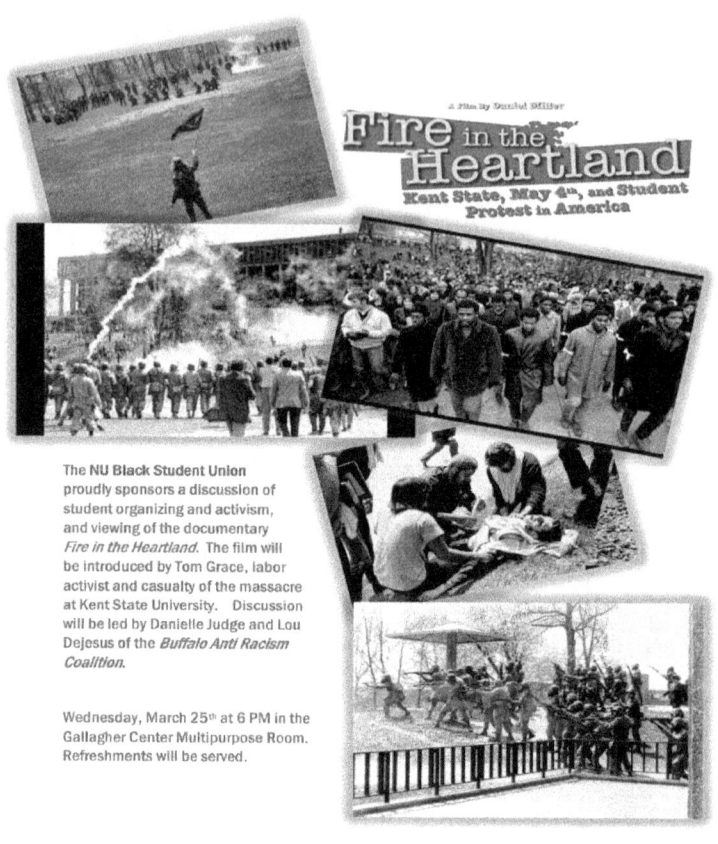

The NU Black Student Union proudly sponsors a discussion of student organizing and activism, and viewing of the documentary *Fire in the Heartland*. The film will be introduced by Tom Grace, labor activist and casualty of the massacre at Kent State University. Discussion will be led by Danielle Judge and Lou DeJesus of the *Buffalo Anti Racism Coalition*.

Wednesday, March 25th at 6 PM in the Gallagher Center Multipurpose Room. Refreshments will be served.

In this respect, one of the reasons historical wounds remain open in America is its perpetual disrespect and lack of acknowledge for the dead. From those who have died from the genocide of our Indigenous People, Blacks who were brought here and enslaved [Maafa], Interment Camps of the Japanese, southern Americans after the Civil War, Immigrants in the 1900's and of course present day Middle Easterners/Muslims and Southeast Asians. I recently attended a viewing/discussion of the documentary Fire in the Heartland at Niagara University by its BSU. Fire in the Heartland is about the National Guard's murder/wounding of Kent State students [May 4 Massacre] and the history of student protests in America. One of the most reprehensible parts of this story was how Kent State and United State Government disrespectfully handling the deaths of the fours students and nine who were wounded -one who suffered permanent paralysis. President Nixon issued a statement which read in part, "This should remind us all once again that when dissent turns to violence it invites tragedy." The problem with his statement was that the protest on that day on May 4th was peaceful and there are images and file footage to prove that. It took nearly twenty years, the 1990's, to even erect some sort of Kent State Memorial in remembrance of this horrible incident and even then there was controversy. This, including the Jackson State Murders; where two students were shot and twelve wounded by the police as they peacefully protested the Vietnam War and United States invasion of Cambodia reflect a systemic attitude in America about death. The death of those who are not viewed as Americans. Fast forward to the incidents of violence by local/state/federal law enforcement agencies against protesters and the handling of the dead surrounding the Occupy Wall Street, Ferguson and etc. and you'll see this clear pattern.

All of this begs the questions we can only answer for ourselves: When there is clear disrespect for the dead, how can there be respect for the living? If our ancestors are not buried [resting] in peace, how can we live in peace? All of us have family and friends who have passed away. Some of us may still be grieving behind their passing and how their burial was handled. Healing those wounds and bringing closure may require us to invest in a reinterment process; beginning with openly talking about that grief or feelings of disrespect, and working together to strive to reconcile those issues.

"It's not you, it's me"

For those of you who didn't know, I facilitate a youth mentor program called STYA which is an acronym for 'Successfully Transitioning Youth to Adolescence.' My demographic are nine to twelve year old's and we do everything from critically analyze cartoons, arts & crafts, cooking classes and etc. to encourage them to expand their consciousness, build self esteem and discover their purpose in life as they transition into their teenage years. What I love most about working with youth, which I've done with various programs and initiatives for over a decade, is learning ideas, attitudes and behavior adults have in their infancy. In other words, I see nine year old girls learning to play the "make a boy jealous" game that eventually becomes a fully functioning operating system I see thirty something year old's use every day. Some things don't change, people just get older and continue doing the same thing. And the same way jealousy games may not change among females, some male's level of sophistication to appropriately respond to these games doesn't change either. I can't tell you how many times I've had to talk a ten year old boy down from an emotional ledge because some little girl was playing with his emotions. His reaction is no different than seeing emotionally unstable men committing social media seppuku because of what some female is, or isn't, posting on Facebook. Some of us simply never matured intellectually or emotionally; we're just older versions of the same child.

Because my Ole Earth was a psychologist/sociologist I've been orientated to analyze human behavior my entire life, literally. Normal family outings were going to places just to people watch; my Ole Earth would find a public place to sit with some of my siblings and I and we would discuss what we see in people's body language, style of dress and etc. One of the games she would also play with us was the book of questions -which I discovered later in life was a psychology book, not a game at all. This kind of investment into my growth and development as a child, coupled with the cultural contributions of my Ole Dad, has helped in my successful transition from boy to man. Some males never had a mother invested in them in this way nor did they have a father around to teach him what it means to be a man. Because of this, some of us have manufactured our idea of manhood 'a la carte' and the emotions and intellect surrounding this lacking remain raw, immature and underdeveloped. This is not an excuse, it's an assessment of what I've witnessed in its infancy and what it has the potential to become when it's not responsibly addressed as an adult. Ladies, young boys may destroy toys when they don't get their way. The same boy who doesn't get his way as a grown male, will destroy you. There's a lot of truth in what Drake says about these days in his song "Own It (Nothing Was The Same)".

Like with any group or society of people, some of its members are going to be emotionally and intellectual immature. One of the challenges I've dealt with over the years are these same boys/girls, not yet men/women, referring to themselves as Gods/Earths. Thankfully this doesn't reflect the overall consciousness of Five Percenters I know, yet there are some of us who are like that -sometimes for reasons only known to them. This is the reason I wrote the book Explorations of God/Earth

Mental Health; to empower my peers to recognize and address it. Because one of our cultural mottos are "Peace" or Positive 'Education Always Corrects Errors', we've always encouraged each other to grow and develop beyond whatever circumstance we've come from or are presently in. For any of us who are sincerely striving to elevate their consciousness and condition, it's a journey that involves removing the negative residue that comes along with seeing and believing ourselves to be inferior. All of us who have taken this step to gain KOS [Knowledge of Self] started out emotionally and intellectually immature. On many levels we're rewiring ourselves emotionally and intellectually and that takes work, sometimes a lifetime. Nothing happens over night, except the night -especially not the growth and development process.

In closing, I want to reiterate the importance of us men getting ourselves together. This is not to minimize the responsibility of grown females who need to grow up either. There are women I know who are successfully speaking from this perspective. As men, we can start getting ourselves together by being more vulnerable with one another by speaking honestly about our upbringing and emotions. I'm not talking about ranting, posturing or posting inappropriate stuff on social media under the guise of "keeping sh#t real"; that's immature and messy. I'm talking about investing the time to really examine who, what, when, where, how and why we think/behave the way we do with each other and the opposite sex. That is one of the most integral parts of KOS. Females share and are vulnerable with each other all the time. That female-to-female educator-to-student relationship directly, or indirectly, has remained pretty much intact since we've been in this country. Males are the one's usually holding stuff in and back from one another. Some of us males were grown up before we had an open conversation with men about hurt, lost, frustration, insecurities, inadequacies, embarrassing situations and etc. Even though some of us aren't sharing these things with each other in a healthy way, it always come out in the most unhealthy of ways -whether that's throwing tantrums or shade, being abusive, gossiping, broadcasting how great we are, taking serial selfies, being a whore or etc. Additionally, there are some things we've experienced as boys that we decided to take with us to our grave. Part of the emotional frustration or indifference you see us express is us trying to live with that lifelong decision. So ladies, when some grown males tell you, "It's not you, it's me", believe it! Also believe the likelihood that they haven't said or done anything about it for over twenty something years and don't plan on saying or doing anything about it after telling you that. We got work to do in order to help get our families/communities back in order and emotional instability and intellectual immaturity won't get us there. As civilized men who advocate righteousness, as Five Percenters and definitely as Gods, we must expect more from ourselves, and each other, to get that job done.

"Jung" Money Cash Money Billionaires

When it comes to being "conscious" and ultimately "consciousness", one thing I've begun to realize is that many of the ideas we have are set upon Sigmund Freud and Carl Jung foundations. Much of our language, analysis, and descriptions of the phenomenon called consciousness, are directly from the books of these 19th Century theorists. Even much of our pedagogy, or method we use to teach about consciousness, is based solely upon Freudian and Jungian psychology. The error in this is not because they're cited. Some of what they taught I agree with. The error lies in the fact that although first world people have been successfully analyzing, articulating, and defining consciousness for thousands of years before both of these men existed, some of us have not taken the initiative to investigate these classical perspectives before drawing a conclusion on what consciousness is, isn't, or even if the word itself is accurate enough to use in order to define this phenomenon.

How we view consciousness sets the stage for our cosmology; our creation story and how we perceive the universe came to exist. This is the basis of our ontology; our sense of beingness, or what it means to be/exist in this universe. Our ontology paves the way for our epistemology, how we come to know things, and our axiology, how we establish our value system. Yet central to all of this 'ology', is our fundamental idea of a/the creator, our relationship to that creator, and our relationship to the earth. If we view consciousness as our brain, this perspective plays a key role in influencing how we process our life experiences. If we view consciousness as having a subconscious and equate this with gender (male and/or female), this will likewise influence our values, and how we interact with others. If we view consciousness as having several different levels, this will likewise influence how we attend this world. How we think influences our way of life.

Carl Jung's definition of consciousness is "*bringing parts of the collective unconscious into ego awareness. Becoming more aware of the workings of the psyche and the meaning of individuation.*" The collective unconscious, according to Jung, is "*the realm of the archetypes including the Self. Ancestral memories and religious instinct reside here as well.*" In layman's terms, Jung viewed consciousness as a process of becoming more aware of the total conscious mind -which consists of discriminating its individual parts. These parts of the conscious mind, according to Jung, are archetypes (inborn pre-formed structures), ideas, memories, instincts, and the Self (guiding center of the psyche or God-image).

You probably have to re-read the above paragraph a couple times if you didn't get it. I wasn't getting it the first time I studied Jung either because it's just plan complicated. Well the key points to keep in mind about Jung's theory are:

* Consciousness is not a state, but a process.

* That process is a method to discriminate components of the conscious mind in order to develop as an individual.

Now that you know this, you can see where many people get some of their ideas about components of the conscious mind (i.e. unconscious, subconscious, super conscious, magnetic conscious and etc.) from, and their quest for individualism (discrimination). It's textbook Jung -with very few, if any, references to first world people's perspective on consciousness. Again, my concern is not with referencing Jung, it's with using Jung as the authoritarian on consciousness. Let us take a moment to analyze a few of his quotes to give you a better idea of what I mean.

"There is no coming to consciousness without pain."

Really? So those of us who buy this believe that unless it's painful, it's not an individual growth and development process. Sounds a little masochistic to me.

"Man's task is to become conscious of the contents that press upward from the unconscious."

Here is one of the biggest departures from how first world people generally define consciousness in comparison to what Jung suggests here. Since the times of Ancient Khemet/Kemet (Egypt) this is what we've taught: ALL is consciousness; undifferentiated matter energy with no variation, vector, or distinction. The term cubconscious or unconscious is really a misnomer because ESSENTIALLY there is no below (sub), above, or around the ALL. Subconscious is a phrase that only applies in the context of the physical realm, where duality, and the denseness of consciousness exists. Consciousness, as an essential state, is all encompassing; omnipresent and omniscient. Our physical vehicle, as a three dimensional conduit and lens of consciousness, only "perceives" and interprets consciousness as various streams. So ultimately, what people call subconscious, unconscious, super conscious, magnetic conscious, or etc. is actually just ALL consciousness. Our physical form, as well as time and space, are filters (conduits) of consciousness. The same way there is relative truth to the denseness and dimensions of the objects around us, in essence, they're ALL one materially (atomically). Consciousness is the same way essentially.

In regards to the term unconscious the only state that could be considered a dynamic opposite of consciousness is 'nothingness' (no-thingness). The negative prefix "un" meaning 'not', as in unconscious (not conscious), cannot be the source of, or proceed, consciousness. Essentially, the only state that is 'not' consciousness is nothingness (no-thingness). Since the creation of this universe, everything that was, is, and will be is an aspect of the ALL -there is no undoing that. Regardless what we choose to believe, there is no 366 degrees, or something outside of the ALL (360 degrees). The ALL was first symbolized as a black dot: "O", a cipher/circle. That glyph/concept of completion represents no-thingness, and everything, simultaneously. A cipher/circle is 360 degrees. 3+6+0 = 9, and everything that was, is, and will be goes through a gestation phase, from no-thingness (0) to something (0), in order to be born complete. That phase is no different than the 9 month process it takes to birth a child. This is also the reasoning behind the glyph/concept "9" being shaped like a spiral, shown to wind around a fixed center point at a continuously increasing or decreasing distance from that point. Therefore, "9" is shaped like a coil circling around that point (black dot; 0), or demonstrates the phase from no-thingness (0) to something (0).

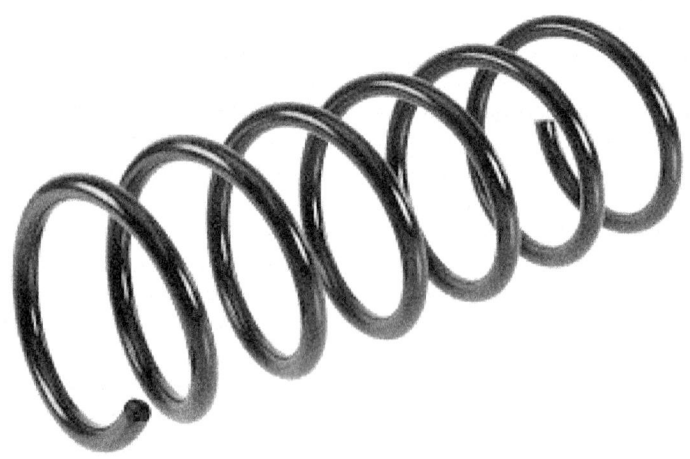

Can you see the number "9" within this circular (0) coil?

Again, the error arises when people only critique consciousness from the vantage point (lens) of their physical form. So because the body serves as a liaison between the intangible (consciousness) and the tangible (material world), people only perceive what they call unconscious (not conscious). So I would argue that man's task is not about becoming conscious of the contents that press upward from the unconscious. Our task is to first realize that consciousness, as an ALL encompassing state, has no below (sub), above, around, or "upward from" it. And everything that our physical form experiences in this material dimension, within these perimeters of time and space, is consciousness -the ALL- being filtered.

Now what does this have to do with money? How we view consciousness directs how we ultimately live, and how we live includes our basic spending habits. Money is what it is and does not equate to an economy. An economy is the systematic, organized utilization of shared resources that can include money, yet money isn't necessary to have a well functioning economy. As a matter of fact, economies have functioned, and still function in some societies, where money didn't/doesn't exist. So the true basis of any economy is how we relate to each other. It's about relating in a systematic, organized way to share resources in order to sustain each other. This means the people who are working to establish, and maintain, an economy must share a collective consciousness, that collective consciousness can be distilled into one practical word: culture.

Culture is the sum total of all of our people activities, and these activities are based upon the principles we adhere to, and values we carry. Our culture is our diet, how we define gender roles, our style of dress, our views on education, the way we rear children and define family units, and etc. Culture either reinforces or undermines the collective consciousness we need in order to establish an economy. One of the main reasons a local economy is generally absent within black/brown and poor white communities as a whole, across the United States, and in areas abroad, is because we lack a collective consciousness, based upon cultural cohesiveness. There are countless examples of people working as a group to empower themselves economically, and this is because they share a cultural basis. They have a common language, heritage, principles, similar experiences, and shared values. These people activities form the cohesiveness necessary to trust, depend upon, and work with one another to preserve, protect, and advance the group. Without this, there is no group reality, sense of community, unified families, or relationships breed division/dysfunction. While many of us are personally looking for money to change our circumstances, we're squandering our cultural capital that will transform our collective condition.

One of the challenges with black/brown people is the fact that many of us live within societies as a subculture, where our point of view isn't primary, nor the consensus of the dominant society. What this means is that what we're taught about life, including consciousness, is filtered through the lens of that dominant society. And that dominant society either reflects an American perspective that's only 237 years old, or it's primarily derived from Greco-Roman perspectives that don't exceed 2,650 years. Although there were many positive observations and contributions made during this segment of time, you'd be hard pressed to find them more in abundance then the observations and contributions that first world people shared over the last 200,000 years, when the world was black. We must not limit ourselves to 237 years, 2,650 years, or even 200,000 years of observations and contributions. We also must not limit ourselves to the theories, and language of 19th Century psychologists when consciousness was well thought out for thousands of years before them, in various geographic locations, by first world people.

We think how we spend, and this thought process is the basis of our economy. When we view consciousness as our ancestors did, as ALL, than we relate to each other collectively -as various manifestations of the ALL. Therefore, we strive to identify with and be sensitive to the common language, heritage, similar experiences, and values we share as one people. As I stated, these people activities form the cohesiveness necessary to trust, depend upon, and work with each other. Wealth is not, and has never been, an individual accomplishment we're led to believe in (i.e. Oprah, Jay Z, Diddy, Tyler Perry and etc.). It is collective work and responsibility. To believe otherwise only serves to enrich those who know they didn't get wealthy on their own. Oftentimes that wealth is old blood blue money, that's been passed down from family generations. So while we're steady trying to make it on our own, as a solo artist for example, we're being used for a tool, and also as a slave, to make money for family businesses, and corporations, we're not a part of. As far as consciousness is concerned, YMCMB is really young money. The driving force behind it is really JMCMB: [Carl] Jung Money Cash Money Billionaires. At the end of the day, Carl Jung's ideas about "ego awareness" and "individuation" are some of the central themes that keep the dominant society's well oiled machine called capitalism going -because many of us buy into it, in more ways than one.

Fasting Breaks The Chains

"If we're not driving, we're being driven." -Saladin

One thing I encourage anyone to do, that is seeking advice about personal empowerment, and maintaining a consistent path, is to master their physical/sexual appetite. It's because of some of our diets, the frequency of our meals, food combination choices, sexual patterns, and lack of activity that most of our energy (life force) is allocated towards our digestive and reproductive systems; the central part of our physical body, and our center of gravity. Our center of gravity is the point of greatest importance, interest, or activity. This is the focal point of our stability, balance, sense of equilibrium, and causation (creation). When we don't possess control of this central part of our being, somebody else will -through appealing to our physical/sexual appetite. When most of our energy is allocated towards our digestive/reproductive systems, other systems in our life get neglected: spiritual systems, economic systems, social systems, educational systems, and etc. They get neglected because we simply don't have the energy to invest in them.

One of the best ways to start gaining control over our physical/sexual appetite is learning how to "fast" (abstain). Fasting helps us master our center of gravity, and gives us an opportunity to redistribute our digestive/reproductive energy to other areas (systems) in our life. Some of the meals we eat, especially 3 in a day, is equivalent to making our digestive system work a 24hr shift. Some of our lives revolve around sex. In conclusion, keep in mind that it's nearly impossible to be personally empowered, and maintain a consistent path in life, when our appetite is driving us. Especially in a society where our appetite is being constantly bombarded with billions of dollars of advertisements of people, places, and things that are designed to appeal to, and control, our life (force). This is not an appeal to become a monk/nun. This is about the benefits of fasting. If we're not driving, we're being driven.

"I'm not into politics"

Them: *"I'm not into politics."*
Me: *"Oh that's alright, politics are in you."*

Running for public office has been one of the most educational experiences in my life. Not just on the 'politician' side, but also what I'm learning about the politics of people, places, and things. Since announcing my candidacy for Niagara County Legislature on July 4th, 2013, I am now about three months into this election year. That's three months of campaigning, learning, and gaining valuable experience about a terrain that's not reflected on a map.

On Tuesday September 10th we had our Primary Election, and the unofficial results show that I won the Working Families party line endorsement. This means that in our November 5th General Election, I will be on the ballot representing 3 party lines; our Niagara Youth Party that I created, the Working Families, and the Green Party. The unofficial results for the Democratic Primary show that I got about 25% of the vote with a write-in campaign; a voter turn-out that has never happened in our district before. People were being told by poll workers that they could only mark the bubble for the candidate on the ballot because the ballots are jamming the machines, others didn't know how to spell my name correctly, some simply marked an "X" in the write-in spot, and still others just voted for the other candidate simply because they were confused about how to do a write-in vote. I was speaking to a woman at a polling site and after she voted she came right outside and told me that she didn't vote for me because she wasn't sure about who I was and what I've been doing in our community. After a few moments of talking she realized that I was a guest speaker at her church Christ Redemption Tabernacle for a Black History Month Program a couple of years ago. She also reminded me that I had given her the framed picture of Jesus and his disciples found in the catacombs of Domitilla Rome, that she proudly has on her wall and she sees every day. All of these challenges I saw and heard personally, or voters shared with me about their experience at the polls. And despite these challenges, without one lawn sign, house mailers, media coverage, or etc. our voter turn-out was a great success.

As I mentioned, one of the most educational parts of this whole experience is what I've been learning about the politics of people, places, and things. See, people are often under the impression that "politics" is an isolated world that people called "politicians" are associated with. The reality is, everything is political. Politics, by one definition, simply means "the science of power or influence." Science comes from the latin root 'scire' which means "to know", so everyone, on some level, even a baby crying for milk, knows how to use power to influence their environment. The clothes you chose to wear today arc influential. The music you like has the power to persuade (influence). Every advertisement we see has a political aim, whether it's influencing us to buy food, get a flu shot, or watch a new sitcom. The reason celebrities do or don't speak about certain current events is political; they may not want to lose endorsements, they may been looking for endorsements, or there may be some other reason. Whether we know it or not, every person, place, or thing in this Interdependent Universe has a fundamental influence, a matrix, and that power was forged through a political process. What does this mean locally? What this means is that the less aware we are of our personal/collective power to influence our environment, our community, and our families, the more power we relinquish, by default; thus allowing others to influence our environment, community, and families for us. More times than not, those who we allow to influence the needs of our environment, community, and families, in a public official capacity, end up using this power to advance only themselves, or use this influence to only help their family. Hence why we have the common phrase, "politics are dirty", which I don't agree with. The way people use politics can be dirty and our city has seen a lot of that over the years.

In closing, I want to reiterate that "politics" are not an isolated world that people called "politicians" are associated with. Everything is political and was forged through a political process. The same politics some politicians use to enrich themselves in office, are the same politics some pastors use to enrich themselves in the pulpit. The same power of persuasion some politicians use to get voters to accept a resolution, is the same power of persuasion some employers use to get employees to accept a policy. The same influence a politician has to positively or negatively impact the district they serve, is the same influence a teacher has to positively or negatively impact the students they serve. For those of you who claim you don't get involved in politics, that idea of neutrality doesn't change the fact that you already are involved, and living on a local political landscape where the decisions of others impact your life each and every day. You mind as well find out more about the people making these decisions, their reasoning for doing it, and if these decisions are helping serve the needs of the community you live in. If not, then you do have the power to personally/collectively change that.

Ms. "Jordan" Ladd

Every "Jordan" Doesn't
Play Basketball

Since putting out my FULL PRESS RELEASE I've monitored the various local news sources to see how they'd cover the story. Not one of them have printed my press release in its entirety. All of them took only parts of it, put their own spin on it, and gave it back to the public the way they saw fit. While I do appreciate some of the publicity, there are other things I saw that were completely inaccurate. Now, The Niagara Falls Reporter printed, and I quote, "*Allah is a convert to Islam and changed his name as is customary for Muslims converts.*"

I am not sure where they got this from. I never spoke to anyone from The Niagara Falls Reporter about the weather let alone religion. I never said that, it's not in my press release, it's not in anything I've published online, and it is completely inaccurate. I am not Muslim nor was my name change for religious reasons. The Niagara Falls Reporter did accurately state, "*Allah says his ancestor was Rev. Josiah Henson, who is said to be the inspiration for the fugitive slave in 'Uncle Tom's Cabin'.*" Yet it's this very part of my ancestry that would have given them more insight about me, my family background, and my name change if they asked me. Since they didn't, I can tell you directly.

Falls woman ties roots to original 'Uncle Tom'

By SUSAN MIKULA CAMPBELL
Niagara Gazette

Inez Dorsey Frank, 78, of Niagara Falls, didn't know until about eight years ago that she was related to one of the more famous passengers on the Underground Railroad.

A cousin told her that she is a great-granddaughter of the Rev. Josiah Henson. Henson is believed to be the model for Uncle Tom in Harriet Beecher Stowe's 19th century anti-slavery novel, "Uncle Tom's Cabin."

"It's something that people didn't seem to talk about. Now a lot of people are trying to find out about the roots of their family," Mrs. Frank said.

Henson was born a slave near Port Tobacco, Md. His father was taken from the family and sold. Henson also was sold away from his mother but they were later reunited.

He was ordained as a preacher by the Methodist Episcopal Church in 1828. In 1830, suspecting that he was to be sold away from his wife and children, Henson escaped with them to Canada.

In 1841, he and a group of abolitionists bought 200 acres of land in Dresden, Ont., and established a school for escaped slaves called the British American Institute. Part of the property is now a historic site. Visitors can see Henson's cabin, grave, a sawmill and other buildings and items used by the original black settlers.

In 1849, Henson was in Boston and dictated his autobiography, "The Life of Josiah Henson, Formerly a Slave." While in that city, he met Harriet Beecher Stowe and told her of his life as a slave.

Henson's daughter settled in St. Catharines and married former slave Allen Alexander Dorsey.

Mrs. Frank moved to Niagara Falls from Canada with her mother in 1925. Mrs. Frank's cousin, the late Gertrude Dorsey of St. Catharines, mentioned their famous ancestor in conversation one day about eight years ago.

Mrs. Frank has never read "Uncle Tom's Cabin" but she visited the Dresden historic site three years ago on a trip organized by her daughter, Edith Garrison of Buffalo.

"It was quite a thrill to see," she said.

Although she said knowing she is related to Henson gives her a nice feeling, she finds more pride in being elected mother of the year by her church and the knowledge that her daughter went back to school after 20 years and is now a Buffalo teacher.

Mrs. Frank said she really hasn't experienced prejudice.

"No matter where you go, there's always some smart alecks," she said.

Mrs. Garrison hopes to organize another trip to Dresden for her mother and other family members.

"It was good to see where we came from and understand we had no reason to walk with our heads down," she said.

RON SCHIFFERLE — Niagara Gazette

Inez Frank of Niagara Falls takes pride in knowing she is a descendant of the Rev. Josiah Henson, a former slave who reportedly inspired the central character in the novel "Uncle Tom's Cabin."

Niagara Gazette article about my Grandmother Inez Frank (1986)

When some of my ancestors were brought to America during the trans-atlantic slave trade, they were enslaved and forced to give up their cultural identity, regardless of their religious ideology. They no longer were allowed to speak their own language, use their own names, maintain the same diet, or even establish stable family units. This process continued, by law, for approximately nine generations or three hundred and ten years. So while some people of Italian descent can trace their last name to an actual village in modern day Italy, or others can trace their lineage to a family crest or coat of arms, tracing my lineage has consisted of looking at cargo logs for ships or doing DNA tracking to find out the geographic location of my ancestors. The trans-atlantic slave trade, and slavery, interrupted the cultural identity and arrested the development of an entire group people. It interrupted the cultural identity and arrested the development of the people enslaved and the slave holders.

In indigenous societies of the past and today, our birth names where a central part of our cultural identity and role we played within our societies. For example, when a child was born a name would be given to them, usually by our elders, to communicate a part of that child's purpose and destiny. This was sacred and ceremonial, not done without consideration. If the child's name meant "sincere counsel", that was an important role our elders knew our society needed to birth and cultivate. It's no different than people giving birth to a child and providing them with all the support and resources they need to become a productive member of society. Many of our ancestors wisely took it a step further by making sure this support was reinforced by a person's actual name. So instead of simply providing a child with the resources to become sincere counsel, we gave them that name to live up to as an attribute. During slavery this cultural tradition was interrupted. Slaves who were bred to produce children for labor no longer had the power to name them. These children were sold off to other plantations and given names to identify them as a master's property. So a slave named "Smith" was identified as Master Smith's slave. "Walking Henson" was known as Henson's slave who walked alot. Not only was this naming method used to track the slave masters property, but it was also used for insurance purposes. There are many wealthy companies and families today that accumulated their wealth, from slave insurances.

Many present day African-Americans can trace the last names we currently have, whether it's English, French, or etc. directly to the slave masters who once owned our ancestors. Again, regardless of our ancestor's religious views or how we chose to worship, this slavery system legally interrupted our cultural identity and arrested the development of us all.

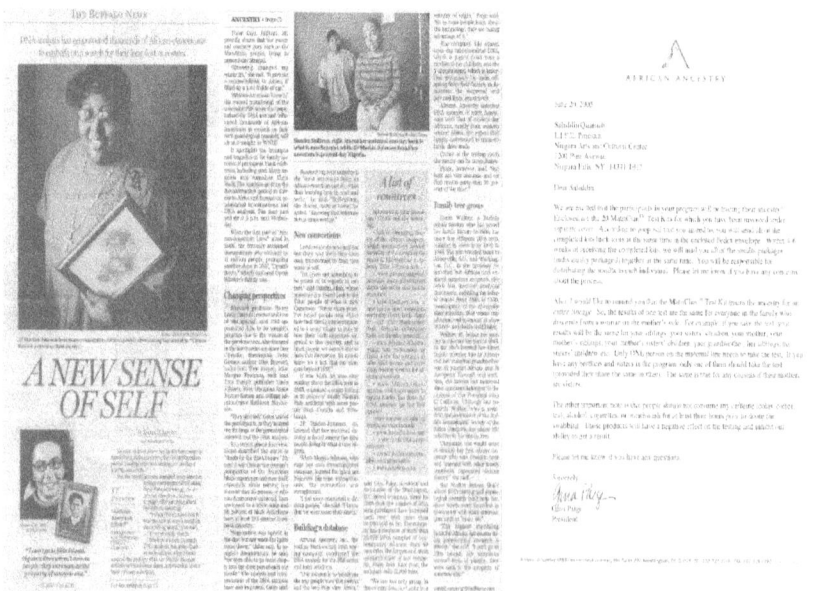

Article in the Buffalo News and letter from African Ancestry Inc. about my International Family Tree Project (2005)

The reason I legally changed my name was to reconnect to my ancestor's cultural identity, and build upon this rich legacy that was almost entirely destroyed. In 2005 I received a grant for my L.I.F.E. Afterschool Program and partnered with the Washington DC based genetics company African Ancestry Inc. to create an International Family Tree Project. With this project I was able to provide twenty DNA kits, free of charge, to families in our Community, Pittsburgh, Missouri, and Canada who were interested in finding out where their maternal ancestry came from. I found out my maternal ancestors came from Cameroon and my tribal affiliation is the Tikar Tribe. Saladin, pronounced Sa-la-dean means "honor or righteousness of the faith". A great Muslim King popularized this Arabic name, yet the name is Arabic, not Muslim. Arabic does not equal Muslim and to assume that would be no different than assuming my nephew plays basketball just because he has the name "Jordan." My middle name Quanaah, pronounced Kwa-ni-ah means "fragrant." In honor of my indigenous (Native American) ancestry, I chose this name. It's Quahadi in origin and comes from the last Comanche Chief Quanah Parker; who successfully made the transition from Chief to Statesman and was responsible for founding The Native American Church. My last name, Allah, is also Arabic which means "The God." Again, Arabic does not equal Muslim. There are many Arabic speaking Christians and other religions who refer to God as Allah, simply because they speak the Arabic language. So my name, Saladin Quanaah Allah, means "The honorable faith and fragrance of the God." Since taking this step to change my name in 1999, I have since published a book entitled 'How To Change Your Name Without A Lawyer' and have assisted many others change their name for various reasons (cultural, religious, stage name, immigrants and etc.)

In closing, I didn't appreciate the Niagara Falls Reporter for even citing what they believe my religion to be; making an assumption about what it is and then printing misinformation without even asking me about my worldview or my reasoning for changing my name. That was poor reporting and prejudiced. I am a scientist of life and study all religions. I am just as much Muslim as our commander and chief: President Barack Hussein Obama. My perspective about any religion is that people should strive to have a personal relationship with who they worship. A relationship that's so personal, that they strive to live in such a way that others can see their creator within them.

Within The Five Percent

One of the common phrases you may hear within the media are "Talking Points." A talking point is a statement designed to support one side taken on an issue during a debate or discourse. It's also a position someone takes or a series of points/remarks used to guide their conversation and support their argument or discussion. Take for example Bill O'Reilly's Talking Points Memo on Fox News. He starts off his memo with a question and then goes into some commentary highlighting different talking points to support his argument. Here's a good example of one of his memos about The Dramatic Muslim Invasion.

What some of us overlook about shows like Bill O'Reilly's Talking Points Memo is that the network itself defines and supports his points/remarks. As a television host on this network, O'Reilly and his points/remarks are used to advocate the network's perspective and vision of the world, the people in it and their relationship to the planet. And when I say "the network's perspective", I'm referring to FNC [Fox News Channel] founders Rupert Murdoch, Republican Party media consultant and NBC executive Roger Ailes and others who own a piece of the company and its sister channels. When we're watching Fox News or any other channel for that matter, their points/remarks are designed to guide their audiences arguments or discussions on that subject matter. Even if we're watching the National Geographic channel; if it's a show about endangered baleen whales, the points/remarks made in that show are designed to guide our arguments or discussions on that subject matter or to possibly solicit financial support from us. When we don't own or control our own media outlets, we don't control our narrative or talking points. And when we don't control our talking points we're subject to others talking about and for us.

When we're having a discussion, engaged in a debate or even an argument, we're exchanging talking points. We're making a series of points/remarks to guide that conversation and support our argument. All of us do it; some do it better than others. However, the goal is not to simply make points/remarks. The goal is to do something with the points/remarks we've exchanged. Generally speaking, Christian talking points are derived from the bible. Muslims get their talking points from the Koran while others include talking points from Muhammad. I know some teenagers who get their talking points from trap music and elementary school youth who get their talking points from the Disney channel, internet and their peers. One time I was asked about the Five Percenter perspective of God by a Christian brother and I simply said, "WWGD: What Would God Do?" I went on to explain that as the biblical scriptures say we are fashioned in the image and likeness of God, our perspective is to strive to do things in a Godly way. He didn't argue with that and I successfully used a talking point not to argue or debate but to guide that discussion in a positive direction, even if that person's intention was to argue or debate.

Within the culture of the Five Percent, 6/8th's or 75% of our talking points are derived from 120 lessons. Our lessons not only define our position on the map of human geography, they contain information that enables us to make a series of points/remarks on an issue, or an aspect of an issue, related to us, our chronology, our relationship to others, the planet and the universe. These points/remarks define our perspective and vision of the world, our discourse at home, in public [abroad] and within the media. If I'm having a discussion with someone about diet, because of my cultural orientation as a Five

Percenter, I may make points/remarks during that conversation that supports a position that they don't embrace, or never heard of before. Whatever those points/remarks are, it's up to me to provide the actual facts and concrete evidence to help them draw their own conclusion. This is the reason I stated 120 lessons is where we get the majority of our talking points from, not Supreme Mathematics. Supreme Mathematics, which is only 12.5% of our cultural curriculum, are principles that correspond to 0-9 within our numerical system; 1 = Knowledge, 2 = Wisdom, 3 = Understanding and etc. Numerals are symbols that represent numbers, they are not numbers themselves. Numerals and Numbers, like the principles of Supreme Mathematics, are abstract concepts/ideas until applied to concrete things. Meaning, Numerals and Numbers, like the principles of Supreme Mathematics, are an idea prior to having a physical or concrete existence. For example, the numeral "3" says nothing concrete in and of itself; it's just a symbol. As the number three, it still says nothing concrete until used to represent "three" apples, for example. In Supreme Mathematics the numeral "3", and number three, corresponds to the principle of "Understanding"; which also says nothing concrete until understanding is explained within the context of every day life. Even if I were to use the common phrase, "The Understanding is the best part; our children," I still have to explain WHAT, WHEN, WHERE, HOW and WHY because that phrase is an abstract concept. Without our explanation, many people don't understand that, will remain confused and oftentimes won't tell you how confused they are; they'll just nod their heads in agreement and won't ask questions for clarity. Mathematics is a mental system that uses numerals as numbers to teach us how to think; how to calculate, quantify and compute reality. Supreme Mathematics is also a mental system that identifies principles that correspond to numerals and numbers that teach us how to calculate, quantify and compute reality. 120 lessons lay out the terrestrial/celestial landscape of the reality we're calculating, quantifying and computing with the principles of Supreme Mathematics and qualities of our Supreme Alphabet.

Consider this: If a person only has the principles of Supreme Mathematics, which are abstract concepts, what is the concrete basis of their talking points? Since their points/remarks are not derived from 120 lessons, where did they get their actual facts from to define their position, support their argument and guide their discussion? Take for example a discussion about the devil, civilization or righteousness which are not any of the principles of Supreme Mathematics. Without 120 lessons, which deal extensively with these subject matters, what is the basis of their talking points about the devil, civilization or righteousness? By simply considering these questions, you can see what's behind some of the contradictory behavior/positions, weak arguments and inability to guide a discussion about our culture by people who claim to be Five Percenters who are not striving to learn 120 lessons and/or who only claim Supreme Mathematics as their entire culture. The same scenario applies to Christians who claim Christianity without knowing the bible, a Tour Guide who doesn't know the area or a Game Stop customer service specialist who is not a gamer. In all of these instances it's only a matter of time before these people sound like they're talking out of their arse, or they look like one, in a discussion.

As Five Percenters, it's impossible to make a consistent series of solid points/remarks to guide our conversation and support our position/argument about this culture if we don't know 120 lessons. We're missing too many points to talk about. Our lessons provide many actual facts about our identity, chronology, the physical dimensions of our planet, our relationships with our human family and the perimeters of our solar system. Again, it's 6/8th's or 75% of our talking points.

September 30th, 1995

Each year I celebrate three different Born Dates: January 6th, April 23rd and September 30th. I was physically incarnated on January 6th. On April 23rd I legally changed my name 16 years ago and have assisted dozens of people do the same via my book How To Change Your Name Without A Lawyer. I celebrate September 30th because on this day in 1995 I finished learning my lessons. In other words, as a Five Percenter I gained KOS [Knowledge Of Self]; I got all 120 lessons from my Enlightener, was tested on my recital and understanding of those lessons and became a qualified Enlightener myself. Since I am 40 years old, this also means that I've been living this way of life half of my life now. From this day forward each year will mean that I've had KOS more years than I haven't. Today I wanted to share some of my thoughts about my experience over the years, where I'm at right now and where I'm aspiring to go.

Like with learning anything new, I had some misconceptions and unreasonable expectations about what gaining KOS and being a Five Percenter was twenty years ago. One of the biggest misconceptions I had was that lessons were something on paper someone hands to you. Even to this day, people with the same misconception reach out to me from all over the world inquiring if I could email, postage mail, inbox and refer them to where they can purchase lessons. When I met my Enlightener and asked him can I get the lessons he didn't write anything down on paper. He developed a companionship with me, we walked together and he taught me the lessons, mathematics and alphabets word of mouth. I eventually wrote them down for myself. The lessons weren't something he handed to me and sent me on my way with. Another misconception I had was the idea that just because I saw the value in this kind of education and journey of KOS that everyone else would too. Not. Lol It took me time to understand and respect that everyone has a choice. I've always been the kind of person who would walk a mile in the snow on a Saturday morning to go to the library. I've also known people who have lived in a city for several years and didn't know for sure where their local library was. I used to judge that, harshly. As I got older and wiser I understood that just because something is meaningful to you it may not mean sh*t to someone else. If someone is interested and invested, they'll strive to do everything in their power to attain it. If not, anything can and will be used to stand in their way. At times I put my own intentions, work ethic and expectations on others. Yes I desired greatness for some and other times it was pure EGO. When it was I learned the hard way that EGO doesn't only Edge God Out of the equation, EGO ultimately Eliminates Great Opportunities to grow, develop and forge healthy relationships. It took me time to understand and respect that everyone doesn't have the same learning styles as well. Some people are visual learners while others are more auditory. Still others are kinesthetic and prefer a hands on approach in education. These were some of the things I didn't know when I first came into the realization of who I was and sought to help others become self actualized.

Anytime we're purposely learning, dealing with and meeting challenges in a white supremacist and institutionalized racist society, it is an accomplishment. There are so many things that can get us caught up, sidetracked, hoodwinked or dead behind. People often compliment me on how graceful, easily understandable and down to earth I present Five Percenter culture. I'm always appreciative of that recognition yet I think it's equally important to recognize that it didn't happen over night. It took and is taking time, patience, sacrifice, studiousness and many other elements to stay the course. In addition to my channel A.S.I.A. TV [www.youtube.com/quanaah], I encourage you to check out my show Atlantis Build Talk Radio to gain further insight about some of these elements, especially Episode 1 Knowledge of Self. In this episode I discuss in more detail my personal growth & development process, the journey of KOS in general and I highlight other significant moments of becoming more self actualized.

In closing, I just want to thank all of you for your continual support and feedback along my journey. Sometimes I look at the clock and wonder how in the world I have enough hours in a day to do the various things I do yet I find a way. My only aspiration is to continue finding ways to further maximize my time and space to do even more. Create more. Be more of an example of Peace. Share more contributions with this world so it's left a better place than when I physically arrived here.

Trumpla: Political Reality TV

While out in DC recently I had the pleasure of running into White House Commentator/Georgetown Adjunct Professor Jon-Christopher Bua. JC covers international politics and writes for a few publications including the UK Huffington Post. We had an excellent discussion on foreign political processes, the 2016 Presidential Election, some of his work media training campaign spokespeople and his course at Georgetown 'Politics and The Media: an American-European Perspective'. One of his latest pieces you should check out is called Donald Trump vs Everyone: Do TV Debates Really Matter and to stay in tune you can follow him on twitter: @JCBua

In a Reality TV society where the best press is bad press, all of this 'Trumpla' and his stagecraft antics have forged him into a one man Morton Downey Jr. show; a true pioneer of political trash tv. Like him or not, the guy is entertaining and represents the voice of millions of Americans who think and feel the exact same way. Like the 1980's era that catapulted Morton Downey Jr. into a pop culture celebrity, the same trend is happening with Donald Trump. To give you a sense of his popular culture impact consider the fact that his name has been dropped in rap lyrics at least 67 times by popular artists over the last 25 years. In terms of popularity, Trump is almost peerless in comparison to other presidential candidates except for Deez Nuts -no pun intended. Unlike Canada or other places where citizens vote for political parties represented by candidates, American citizens vote for the popular guy, not political platforms. Couple that kind of political process with an uneducated apathetic electorate and this is exactly what we see is exactly what we get.

Two things I wanted to point out about Donald Trump is his 'whig' and no nothing political platform. When I say whig I'm not talking about the spider monkey hairpiece on his head. I'm talking about his Whig Party perspectives. In the mid 1800s, the Whig Party were known as American Patriots, anti-Democratic and took many conservative stances that would be considered 'far right' today such as occupational prestige and upper class opportunism. Eventually succeeded by the Republican Party, Whigs were also said to be many things to many people, willing to abandon core convictions for the purpose of gaining political clout. Ironically the word whig is derived from the Scottish word 'whiggamore' and Donald Trump shares Scottish ancestry; his mother Mary Anne MacLeod was from the island of Lewis on the west coast of Scotland. In regards to Trump's no nothing political platform, his views are reflective of The Know Nothing Party's xenophobic (fear or dislike of foreigners/outsiders), anti-immigration/naturalization sentiments. Also active in the mid 1800s, The Know Nothing's were a party who viewed themselves as the true Native Americans and only accepted membership of Protestant males born of British ancestry. They were also considered semi-secret because its members were instructed to reply, "I know nothing" if asked about the Party's activities. Unlike today, xenophobic, anti-immigration/naturalization and anchor baby sentiments are not a secret; every time Trump opens up his mouth it's clear he doesn't 'know nothing' about how to address certain national and foreign policies.

In the final analysis I think it's important that we understand that things happen in cycles, including political philosophies. Technology wise, we just have easier access to some of the same ideologies that built or destroyed this country in the past. In order to be an educated electorate we must be aware of this. I don't have a prediction on the outcome of the 2016 Presidential Election because it's still too early to tell who corporate America will choose to represent their interests. What I will say is that we cannot underestimate the power of popularity vs political platforms. A little over a decade ago the Morton Downey Jr. Show set a rachet television precedence and helped pave the way for reality television. Today we have a new kid on the block leading the same flock and it's going to be hard to trump that.

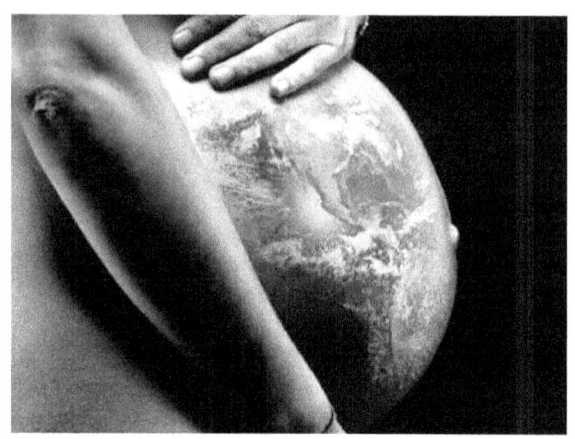

The Original Woman

and

Planet Earth

Within Five Percenter culture, one of the common phrases people may hear us use is, "The original woman [black woman] is the Earth." Have you ever really considered what this means? I once heard a female say, "It means she's dirt", which is as far from the truth as Meek Mill's diss track response to Drake. Anyway, some of my female readers have been reaching out to me requesting that I elaborate on this perspective further and here it is.

We consider the original woman [black woman] the Earth because she corresponds to our planet. Meaning, she is parallel or equivalent to it in form, character and function. When we say 'black' we are referring to all women of color; from the darkest shade of black to the lightest shade of black. As black is the essence from which all color is derived, these melanated shades are gradations of that source. When it comes to geography, the study of describing the Earth, our planet has various shades [gradations] of soil yet it's still one planet. Human [hue-man] geography is likewise the same; as people of color we're one original family. I think it's important to clarify this because some people may think that being dark skinned is what makes us original or first. That is not entirely true because regardless how much melanin we have, we still may be last in a lot of things in life -including intellectual maturity. So in addition to color, we must also consider consciousness and cultural orientation when it comes to what being original means.

Various classical and indigenous societies view the original woman as Mother Earth, the Great Mother and Mother Nature because of her form, character and function -such as her physical composition, atmosphere and ability to birth and sustain life. One of the first things to keep in mind about the Earth is that it's a terrestrial planet. That's where the name 'Earth' is derived; the Latin root "Terra", the root word of terrestrial meaning 'of the land.' This means that our planet possesses a solid surface and a metallic core. This core is the source of Earth's geomagnetic field that shield's it from cosmic radiation. The Earth also has four different layers: an inner core, outer core, mantle and crust [surface]. Lastly, Earth is distinguished from the other terrestrial planets Mercury, Venus and Mars because it possesses water which is vital for life as we know it. All of these qualities have a symbolic relationship to the original woman. In regards to the Earth's primarily Iron [Fe] core, the source of its geomagnetic field that shield's it from cosmic radiation, iron is considered the life-force of the Earth in some societies such as the Aborigines of Australia. As a life-force of the Earth, it symbolizes a woman's vitality, integrity, resilience, strength and fortitude. In regards to functioning as a geomagnetic shield, that symbolizes a woman's protective instinct against outside danger. The four different layers of the Earth symbolize the layers of a woman. The crust is the surface or most outer layer of the Earth. This represents what and how we physically see a woman; this is her appearance. The mantle is the second layer or what lies just beneath the surface; as a mantle is that which cloaks, shrouds or disguises. Also keep in mind that movement of the mantle causes tectonic activity such as volcanic eruptions and earthquakes on the crust, her surface. In symbolic terms, sometimes it's something lying just beneath the surface, undetected by the naked eye, causing the unstable activity we see on the outside. The hottest and deepest layers of the Earth are the outer and inner core which are primarily composed of iron and nickel, thus making the planet magnetic. It is in this interior place that our Earth derives its magnetic field; its North and South Poles [compass]. In symbolic terms, internally is where you'll find the core convictions and source of a woman's moral compass and sense of direction. As the Earth possesses other precious metals and minerals that develop within its womb, women possess the ability to develop precious life within their womb; children. The Earth's weather is primarily determined by the state of its atmosphere, as a woman's mood is partly determined by the state of her emotional atmosphere. The Earth's magnetic relationship with the Moon's 28 day lunar cycle effects our planet's tides the same way a woman's 28 day menstrual cycle effects her emotional tides that are linked to her sympathetic nervous system that partly regulates her hormones and body's ability to cope with stress. As hunter gatherers that eventually transitioned into agriculture and industrialism, we directly consulted with women who were biologically in tune with our landscape, planting and harvest seasons. As forecasters, their wisdom and guidance was critical to our survival and that consultation also corresponds to the creation of calendars based upon a 28 lunar and her 28 day menstrual cycle. Among many societies, a woman is seen as an Oracle [diviner] within its cultural matrix because of her intuition, our southern relatives call "mother wit" and what Western Philosophy has come to define as priori knowledge. In Greece for example, she was the priestess Pythia; central figure of the Gaia [Earth] society and Oracle of Delphi men would consult for guidance on the seventh day of each month.

Women defining themselves as the Earth is not a Five Percenter trademark nor is it our intellectual property. That idea has existed for many years, in different geographic locations and among various societies before there was a North America and the Father was born. Culturally speaking, how we define, articulate and apply that idea as Five Percenters is unique to us, and how we define and articulate those parallels are customarily represented by our women. So for example, as the Earth is covered 3/4th's under water, 139,685,000 square miles of water and 57,255,000 square miles of land, Five Percent women dress modestly; clothing themselves 3/4th's as various other women around the planet likewise do. Something that also distinguishes Earths are the customary head wraps [crowns] they wear. We consider all of this her refinement because that style of dress reflects a sense of decency, cultural elegance, sophistication and grace. To learn more about refinement you can check out the blog of Izayaa Allat. Nutritionally, and to promote optimum health, our women strive to not pollute their bodies the same way many of our ancestors did not pollute, defile or desecrate themselves or the Earth. Therefore, our women strive to make certain dietary choices and engage in those people activities that help them maintain a positive physical, emotional, mental and financial state. As men we strive to reciprocate that state by making corresponding dietary choices and engaging in those people activities that help us maintain a positive physical, emotional, mental and financial relationship with our woman, and the planet Earth. The Earth rotates on its own axis yet revolves around the Sun. The rotation, travelling 1,037 1/3 mph, is symbolic to a woman's autonomy, identity, self-determination and purpose. It's her motion, personally. The Earth's revolution is her motion around another body; her orbital relation to the Sun within the context of our solar system. In symbolic terms, as man corresponds to the Sun, a woman's revolution as the Earth is her interdependent role and relationship within the nuclear family.

These are just a few of the countless examples why we as Five Percenters, and various societies around the world, view the original woman as the Earth's twin. Even if we were to say a woman were a Goddess, as a deity she still maintains a terrestrial correspondence and is personified/defined according to earthen qualities. So there is no way around, below, above or through that; a woman is analogous to the Earth. I think it's also important to note that just because a woman doesn't call herself the Earth within the context of the Five

Percent, it doesn't mean that she's not functionally corresponding to the Earth. There are various indigenous societies who have never heard of Five Percenters that equate their women as the Earth and who've been successfully expressing that worldview for hundreds of years. There are also various women today who live by non-Western cultural norms that are Earth-centered. It's likewise true that just because a woman calls herself the Earth it doesn't mean that she automatically corresponds to that. Some women, and people for that matter, are more aligned than others, regardless what we call or don't call ourselves.

In closing I want to remind those of you who have read this intellectual breakdown of the original woman's correspondence to the Earth that it does not substitute learning from, walking with and having an actual relationship with the true and living Earth. As a male/man, I do not correspond to the Earth and there are many things I am not personally qualified to speak on. That is the role and responsibility of the Earth, not the Sun; I am simply shedding light. So in addition to reading these articles, my books and watching my videos I strongly encourage you, particularly women who are interested in learning more about the Earth, to do so from the true and living Earth. You can email me directly at: atlantisbuild@gmail.com and I can strive to connect you with the sisters I know in your respective regions.

No Sharing

~The Science of Polygamy~

I once had a polygynous relationship for over a year. Polygyny is a form of polygamy where a man has a relationship with two or more women. It wasn't the kind of relationship I sought after or even considered having at the time. The opportunity was presented to me and I agreed. I was young, naive and learning its perimeters in real time. Now let me get this straight from the door, it wasn't a habitat for threesomes nor was I lying in the valley of the skins. That's not the purpose of polygamy; it's much more sophisticated and civil than that, well at least it should be. Polygamy, and polygyny in particular, goes back many centuries to classical and indigenous societies who sought to resolve the growing disparity between male and female ratios, family/community deterioration and moral decay. Depending upon where you went or still go in the world, that human sex ratio disparity can be as large as 12 females to every male or as low as 2 females for every male.

In the United States from the 1950s to the 1990s a Dr. William Masters and his assistant Virginia Johnson pioneered research on human sexual response in the department of Obstetrics and Gynecology at Washington University in St. Louis, Missouri. The significance of their research is that it explored the nature of female arousal and orgasms; which many males knew nothing about or didn't want to know anything about even to this day. From the perspective of this society, "sex" is generally defined as male pleasure and the "sexual act" is considered complete after a male has an orgasm. Like today, and during the time of Masters and Johnson's research, males didn't want to explore or even talk about female arousal and orgasms because our ability to help her achieve sexual arousal and orgasm is called into question. So instead of facing the fact that we may be impotent or simply unable to please a woman, males played, and play, the blame game by calling a woman frigid. This male insecurity runs so deep that even the MPAA [Motion Picture Association of America] rates films pornographic or NC-17 even if a fully clothed woman appears to be experiencing arousal or an orgasm. NC-17 was once called "X-rated" and I encourage you to research NC-17 big box office hits and you'll understand the cultural and socioeconomic impact of such a rating. Not only is it an award season kiss of death but it's a mark against women enjoying sex on film.

Within this society males are socialized to get their rocks off and slut-shame females who are doing the same thing. According to that "get my rocks off" logic, when a female isn't aroused and hasn't reached orgasm, it lowers the chances of having a male child when a male ejaculates inside of her. The alkaline secretions in a female's vagina increases each time she orgasms. This simultaneously decreases its acidic level which is an unfavorable environment for sperm survival; especially Y-chromosome sperm. Also, because healthy cervical mucous of a female is alkaline, if we're daddy long stroke and can use the right sex positions to deposit our sperm inside of the cervix, it's a shorter distance for Y-chromosomes to travel in order to reach the egg. The fact that many females within the United States practice a standard American diet high in meat, dairy, white sugar/high fructose corn syrup, processed foods and few fruits/vegetables makes her body as a whole more acidic than alkaline. This is not to put it all of her because many of us males have a low sperm count for some of the very same dietary reasons, including drug use, alcoholism, erectile dysfunction and of course depression. I mention the research of Masters and Johnson, MPAA film ratings and how female arousal and orgasm plays a role in gender determination to show some of the psychological, sociological and physiological factors that directly effects the human sex ratio.

Now what do these ratios have to do with polygamy? According to human sex ratios, one thing that is generally consistent across the board is that there has been and are more females on the planet Earth than males. When this isn't the case.., where you do see a disproportionate amount of males to females.., it's usually the direct result of conditions such as gendercide, pollution, aging/death rate, poor diet, genetics, sex selective abortions and infanticide. Traditionally, some societies used more humane solutions to bring to balance its human sex ratios where females outnumbered males. In addition to these conditions, two of the main reasons for this disparity in human sex ratios were war-time casualties and short male lifespans that left widows and orphans behind. Polygyny became the first social security system; it provided a safety net for its women and children who had no husband and father. Plural marriage was also established to maintain the moral fabric of the society dealing with these disparities. In many instances where there were not enough available males there was an increase in adultery, lesbianism, prostitution, divorce, alcoholism/drug use, mental illness and other societal ills. All of these social ills erode the moral fabric of any society. Polygyny was a solution to a society where there were more females than males, and even though it was and is well intended, you may not have men of integrity participating in it. This lack of integrity only compounded and compounds the issues of providing social security for our women and children, especially in a patriarchal society.

In many American cities, like in various countries and cities around the world, the odds are against a female finding a single available male companion; we're unavailable, literally. Without understanding these human sex ratios some females may simply be under the impression that males are born cheaters and some females are naturally desperate. Some females may also believe that what I'm saying isn't true and they're going to find a man and have a lifelong monogamous relationship with him. The reality is in a city where there's 6 females to every male, you're most likely to be one of the 5 females who won't have a man; unless of course you openly/privately share him, you make him pay to be with you or you strive to take him from another woman. Some women just decide to be in a relationship with one or more of the other 4 women who are left. That is the reality, regardless how much we pray, hope or believe differently. Keep in mind that there are also societies that practice polyandry. Polyandry, although not as common, is also a form of polygamy where a woman has a relationship with two or more men. This plural marriage was likewise established for the same reasons; to bring into balance the human sex ratio disparity where males outnumber(ed) females. This was also done to help maintain the moral fabric of the society where adultery, homosexuality, prostitution, violence, alcoholism/drug use, mental illness and other societal ills would increase because of the lack of available females.

One of the questions I often ask males who advocate polygamy is, "Do you advocate polyandry as equally important as polygyny?" Some may have never heard of it. Others that have heard of it don't consider it equally important. My perspective is this: If we truly understand the purpose of polygamy, we should have no problem practicing polygyny or polyandry if that's what our society needs to effectively address its human sex ratio disparities, family/community deterioration and moral decay. I'm sure that's a hard pill to swallow for many of us males/men but that's the kind of sacrifice we're asking our women to make for the greater good of maintaining our society. We should likewise be willing to make that same sacrifice if called upon to do it.

As Five Percenters, we like other classical and indigenous societies recognize polygyny as a viable solution to the human sex ratio disparities and moral decay. Even though we recognize plural marriage, it does not mean that all Five Percenters participate in it. When we do, polygyny is a relationship established for the women. It's not supposed to be a man throwing two women together for his personal benefit. It's women coming together as sisters and deciding to share a relationship with a man who is capable of benefiting them, the family and community. The man should be in a position to decide whether that relationship benefits him too, thus benefiting the family and the community. When a woman or women are already willing to have a plural marriage and bring the idea to him, he already knows up front that they have some vested interest in it working out. Everybody is invested. If he comes up with the idea and independently brings it to his woman or women, they don't have the same vested interest in making sure it works out; that's his idea and his responsibility. This can easily become a sabotage scenario. In my experience, it wasn't my idea and I agreed to that relationship when I saw that it benefited all of us. It didn't work out because the first woman, who brought the idea to me in the first place, became insecure within the relationship and decided to end it. I was young and didn't fully understand how to deal with co-Queen rivalry, jealousy, time sharing and other important factors to maintain such a sophisticated relationship.

In today's society we find ourselves dealing with many and more of the exact same problems that polygyny successfully addressed in the past, and still address today. Do I think that this is a viable solution? Partially, yet it's not a silver bullet. With the level of emotional instability, lack of financial literacy/stability, integrity and various other things that plague many of us males, many of us are unprepared to handle such a sophisticated relationship. That is a tragedy because many women are left to their own devices and our families, and communities, suffer behind it. At the same time there are some of us men who are prepared to maintain a polygynous relationship yet many women are unprepared to handle such a sophisticated relationship. Aside from the emotional instability, lack of financial literacy/stability, integrity and etc., some women just don't see other women as sisters to the point where they're willing and able to share this kind of relationship. Even the best of women, including Five Percenters, find it difficult to do this. Whatever the reasoning is, if we're not considering polygyny as a viable solution to the human sex ratio disparities, family/community deterioration and moral decay in our societies, we need to come up with a better idea. Our future generations depend upon it.

Justice or Else: What's Next?
7 Experiences of a Five Percenter

It's 3:09am and I'm up reflecting and writing on the 10.10.15 Justice or Else Rally in Washington DC I recently attended. Although there were many things I saw and heard, here are 7 Experiences I wanted to share with all of you. Before I do that I want to first give a shout out and thank my brother Keith Muhammad of Luv4Self for organizing our trip and the other members of our entourage for travelling down.

- I loved seeing the numerous vendors utilizing this entrepreneurship opportunity to provide goods/services for the people. It was definitely an example of cooperative economics. Aside from the economic stimulus to the city's economy via food, lodging, transportation and etc., I'm already working on something to address and redirect some of that revenue to neglected communities/commercial zones when gatherings like this take place, regardless of the City/State.

- The "Justice or Else: What's Next?" National Community Forum I participated in focused on various grassroot programs, projects and initiatives we're engaged in that already addresses "What's Next?" We discussed the political process, displacement/gentrification, education models, cooperative economics and etc. The best part about grassroot forums such as this is people don't simply leave encouraged. We were there working and we left with tasks. For example, during a segment we took a moment to come up with a vision statement and #hashtags to start tweeting a public official to begin using our social networks to mobilize around a specific quality of life issue. Click the highlighted link so you can check it out.

"Justice or Else: What's Next" National Community Forum

- I'm glad I had an opportunity to connect with so many people in the flesh who are working towards bringing about a better world for our present and future generations. I'm also glad that I was able to connect with my Queens and Howard University students Asiyah and Aziza and share some time with my eldest Asiyah because her 20th Born Day was also 10.10.15. In addition, 10.10.15 marks the 51st year and formal Born Day of the Five Percenters so it was also beautiful to celebrate that with some of my Universal Family. One of my best highlights was finally meeting the young sun my God Brother and his Queen gave me the honor of naming "Khemel." That was indeed love to the highest degree!

185

- By the time I arrived in DC I was running on fumes: the last full meal I had was a day earlier and I hadn't slept in 60 hours. Although I ended up eating some of the food/water donated by Author D. Scott I still hadn't slept taking turns driving back. Not sure if any of you have experienced this before but lack of sleep can make you hallucinate. At one point the white vehicle in front of me turned red and looked like a Dumb & Dumber version of Clifford The Big Red Dog. Lol I say this to say: when you're travelling, make sure you get some rest first and possibly when you arrive somewhere, before you travel back.

- Of the many positive things people said to me, one of the things that struck me was a brother saying how proud he was of me for the way I represent Five Percenters worldwide. It wasn't a back handed compliment and he was sincere about it. I appreciated that because it's not often that brothers put their EGO aside and honestly give another brother credit like that without wrapping it up in joke or mumbling it. Herein lies a greater problem with that mentality: When we're not sharing our love, support and appreciation for each other, we're not showing our younger generations how to love, support and appreciate each other. One of the reasons we don't see it in our millennial generation is because they don't see us doing it. I've not had an issue sharing love, support and appreciation for what others are doing and willfully that gesture symbolizes a growing sense of unity and cooperation we need as brothers to effectively address the problems that are plaguing our families and communities.

- The "or Else" means many things to many people. To me it's an unfinished sentence that represents the consequences of apathy, disunity, egotism and blind consumerism. So for example, "Justice or else... we're going to see the continual deterioration of our families and communities." Sometimes in order to build, some things must be destroyed. In this case, and among other things, it's apathy, disunity, egotism and blind consumerism that must be destroyed in order to transform our present conditions.

- If we're participating in a nationwide blackout/boycott to not support certain businesses and services we also should blackout/boycott promoting and advertising certain businesses and services. For example, not buying Polo gear for a couple of days yet simultaneously posting pictures on Instagram, Twitter and/or Facebook wearing Polo gear defeats the purpose of participating in a blackout/boycott. Even though we didn't buy anything, we may have encouraged half a dozen people to go buy something. Lol Just something to think about. There's a video I published on my youtube channel [www.youtube.com/quanaah] entitled 'Advertising and Self Determination' where I further elaborate on this.

In closing I had an excellent time building and networking with others, seeing the beauty of our unity and leaving with more ideas to continue my work at home and abroad. Regardless who was there, who spoke and etc., people will ultimately take away from this event what they brought to it and willfully what they gained while being there.

Minister Louis Farrakhan

Friend Or Foe?

One week following the 10.10.15 Justice or Else Rally in Washington, DC I couldn't help but notice the widespread criticism of Minister Farrakhan and his Nation of Islam by both mainstream media and the everyday person via their social media page. Some of these criticisms have been outright name calling such as "FarraCON" or 'FarraCoon"; defining the minister as a misleading charlatan that's blood sucking the poor. Others have been less abrasive and have articulated their desire to see the evidence and practical application of "or Else" -which they claim wasn't defined at the rally. In his defense, some of his supporters have retorted that a General doesn't announce his strategies to the public, the minister has laid out plans of action years before the rally and people have no right to question someone in his position because they're not the leader. Well today I wanted to offer a perspective to willfully help reconcile these perspectives.

For those who are Anti-Farrakhan:

First and foremost I think it's important to keep in mind that as a leader, some view the minister as a spiritual father, father figure and ultimately someone who occupies a parental role within their life. Considering this, whatever your criticisms are of him, it sounds and feels no different than you talking about someone's parent. Imagine someone talking about your mother or father. Regardless how respectful or on point someone is with a criticism of your parent, you're going to feel some kind of way about it, initially. I don't know many people who are comfortable with someone calling their parent names, ridiculing them or etc.: those are usually fighting words. Even though no person, parent or not, is above criticism, there's always a certain level of respect we've shown our parents even if they were dead wrong. And when I say respect I don't mean "agree and go along with any and everything they say" because sometimes they're not the best knower in every given life situation. To take it a step further: even though the minister may not look it and he colors his hair, he is an 82 year old grandparent and great-grandparent. That in itself warrants the kind of respect we show any elder, not just a parent. And just like our own grandparents and great-grandparents, we may not agree with everything they're saying or doing, but out of respect, there's a way we should talk to and talk about them. That is the posture, decorum and etiquette of a civilized person.

Because I am a free thinker I don't agree with what everyone says or does. Everyone doesn't always agree with me and there are times I reassess something I said or did and don't agree with myself. That being said, I think it's healthy to express the right to critically analyze what anyone says or does. However, I think we have that right not simply for the purpose of argument or to point out what we think is wrong. We have that right, and responsibility, to show and prove what's wrong by presenting what's right. In other words, if you think I can use a better strategy in my STYA Program to teach my youth, don't just point out what you think I'm doing wrong, offer me the right way. When you approach people by penalizing them, as opposed to offering them an alternative, people tend to shut down and be unreceptive to what you have to say. For example, I also teach preschool in addition to my program and there are times I see my students do something wrong. One day I gave a student instructions on practicing their writing. When I walked over to check their work they weren't following the instructions. They were writing, they just weren't following the right instructions. I didn't walk over, snatch the pencil out of their hand and say, "No, that's not how you do it. This is the right way." I said, acknowledging they were at least writing, "Hey..., that's good. Now see if you can write it this way" as a patted them on the shoulder and redirected them back to the right instructions. As adults the same approach, sense of consideration and tact applies. People are generally more welcoming to being offered alternatives than just being criticized or even ridiculed for what they feel, think or believe. This is not to say that we should not engage in intellectual discourses and tiptoe around everybody. This is to say that the basis of these discourses should not be for the purpose of name calling, to ridicule others or for pissing contests. The purpose of any intellectual discourse, especially with our people, should be to discuss and assess the best ideas and strategies to solve our problems. If someone is so caught up in their feelings that they have an inability to rise above their emotions for that purpose, then you need to walk away. Some people worship who they perceive as their leaders, whether it's Jesus, Muhammad, Beyonce, Buddha, Minister Farrakhan and even The Father Allah. And anything you have critical to say about them will be outright rejected, including you and some of your well meaning uninvolved associates.

For those who are Pro-Farrakhan:

Just because someone questions a man or woman's idea or strategy it doesn't make them an agent, hypocrite, hater or anything else some of you define as antagonistic. Sometimes people simply have and can share a perspective others don't see. This is the reason Minister Farrakhan has a research team;

there are things he simply doesn't know or understand and he relies on a counsel of advisors to teach him. And yes, some of them are about half of his age. Now keep in mind that there are many people who are not a part of the minister's advisor team who are more than qualified to advise him, and them, too. Many of these men and women are not Muslims nor are they registered members of his Nation of Islam. Some of them are a part of your social networks and you interact with them often. I mention this to emphasize the fact that knowledge is inexhaustible which gives everyone the potential of being a best knower in any given situation. Some find it difficult to grasp this reality because it seems to conflict with a hierarchal structure of having one leader at the top and a descending order of roles beneath them. It's difficult to imagine that someone beneath the person at the top can conceptualize something beyond that leader's realm of thinking. It's also difficult to imagine that the person at the top cannot conceptualize something from someone that's beneath them. You are aware that someone had to teach Minister Farrakhan how to set up and use a Twitter account right? I'm sure you also know his team of advisors put him on to certain Rappers he never heard about before because they were key support contacts he needed to meet in order to promote the Justice or Else rally, right? The point in saying this is to remind all of you that the title of leader doesn't mean that someone personally has all of the answers. No great leader would make that claim, and when these leaders do make the honest claim that it's not about them, and even give credit to their benefactors, many of us simply don't believe it.

One of the other things that's important to understand is this: there are those who respectfully disagree with the 10.10.15 Justice or Else rally because they have a hard time "quantifying" it. Sure many can speak about the quality of their personal experience and no one can take that away from them, but how do you accurately quantify or measure that experience? This is one of the reasons some people were/are discouraged and disenchanted with the rally; they don't see a tangible, concrete example of "What's next?" For example, the 2015 BET Hip Hop Awards viewer ratings were down over 50% [1.4 million] this year from 2014. It can be argued that this plunge is a direct result of the BET Boycott social media campaign against the network for not covering the rally. You can even argue how the current nationally conscious #BlackLivesMatter backdrop, coupled with the Justice or Else rally, has created the Anti-Empire sentiments responsible for their weekly rating drop. That is quantifiable, it's tangible and concrete. For those who would like to effectively demonstrate the rally's impact, or even the minister's impact on a local, regional, national or international level, these kinds of quantifiable Talking Points are necessary to show and prove it. Some people are simply not moved by someone's personal beliefs or human interest stories. Understandably, some people want to know what's in it for them, what is the actual outcome, if/when they invest their time and/or money into something.

Hopefully, this will be the year that we cause Santa to commit suicide, along with the racist, money-grubbing profiteers that he helps to keep rich.

No Justice for us.
No Profit$ for them.

NO BLACK FRIDAY.
NO CYBER MONDAY.

BOYCOTT CHRISTMAS
"We must kind of redistribute the pain."—Dr. Martin Luther King, Jr.

In conclusion, I think it's important to keep the focus on the collective movement of people who are actually invested in programs, projects and initiatives to bring about justice. I had an opportunity to participate in a National Community Forum after the rally which echoes these sentiments. It took place at We Act Radio Station [Washington DC] and its purpose was to bring people from across the nation together to discuss these programs, projects and initiatives we're already invested in and how you can also get involved. In addition to checking out the above link for ideas of how you can get involved, here is something else you can do and share with others: Down from 11% last season, we the people are again calling for a Nationwide Boycott during the Holiday season (November – December 2015) to not purchase any goods or services. If anyone makes any purchases, it should be strictly with Black-owned businesses. Also, we are encouraging everyone to not advertise or promote any goods, services, brands/logos of outside companies using their social networks [Instagram, Facebook, Twitter and etc.]. We should only advertise or promote Black-owned businesses. Let's keep our personal beefs and religious disagreements off of social media and at home. Publically we must continue to be positively invested in this collective momentum that's quantifying the transformation we would like to see.

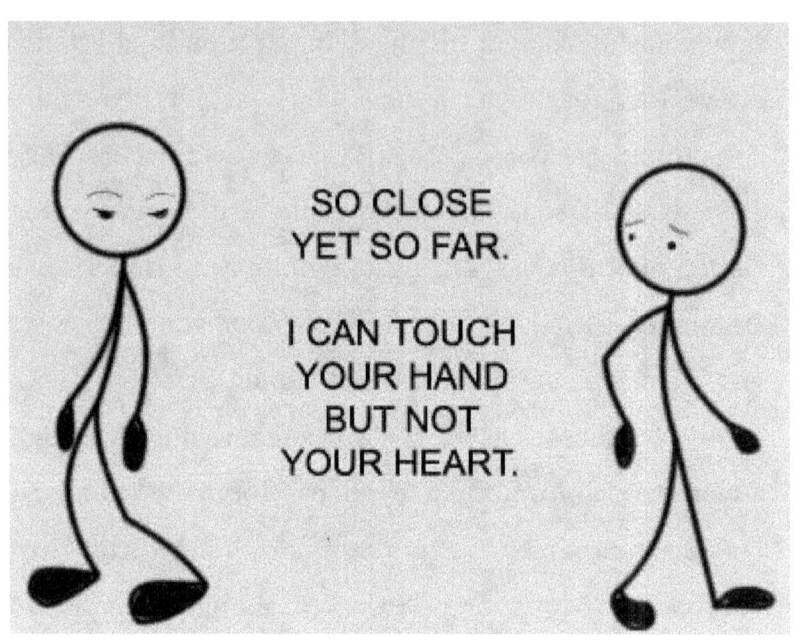

Gamophobia: Unrequited Love

In today's technological age of text messaging, social media and smart phones we have instantaneous access to information, people, places and things unlike ever before. I can literally go online right now and order an item rush delivery from China that will arrive at my doorstep within the week. I talk to my God brother in Ghana like he's next door using a free app and I have successfully hosted a Hip Hop album Unique Heat Vol 3: Clearer Understanding that was produced overseas without me having set foot in the UK. That is convenience. The downside to all of this is the minimization and lost of the human touch. With this lost of a human touch has come chronic and temporary emotional unavailability and people who have Gamophobia; a fear of commitment.

When it comes to emotional unavailability, there are various reasons why people have issues with closeness and intimacy. As elaborated on in my book GAMES, some people have emotional unavailability issues going all the way back to their childhood. These issues, sometimes defined as R.A.D. [Reactive Attachment Disorder], classifies children who have a problem forming meaningful attachments/bonds with others. Scientists examined how the lack of attachment (stroking) that babies received over a period of time made them either not respond or react negatively to social attachments with others. In addition to the emotional, social and cognitive components, this lack of response and/or negative reactions towards attachments was also measured in the low or stabilized levels of Oxytocin these children had during pleasurable inter-activities. Children like this, without the proper counseling, tend to carry this into adulthood. Other reasons some people are emotionally unavailable include, but are not limited to, failed relationships, divorce, [sexual, emotional, physical or financial] abuse, trauma, mental illness, parental alienation, addiction, being workaholics and etc. Whatever the cause may be, the effect is the same; a person's unwillingness or inability to be close to and share space with others. One of the other things that's worth mentioning here in regards to emotional unavailability is the trans-generational trauma First World [Original] People have suffered at the hands of western colonialism, global white supremacy, institutionalization racism and sexism. As a coping mechanism, many of us have learned to not put our thoughts or feelings out there and have been emotionally unavailable to America, so-called Americans and American ideals for generations; our livelihood and survival has depended upon that.

According to Dr. Judith Orloff, psychiatrist/author of Emotional Freedom and other books, the ten key signs that someone is emotionally unavailable are:

1. They are married or in a relationship with someone else.

2. They have one foot on the gas pedal, one foot on the brake.

3. They are emotionally distant, shut down, or can't deal with conflict.

4. They're mainly interested in sex, not relating emotionally or spiritually.

5. They are practicing alcoholics, sex addicts, or substance abusers.

6. They prefer long distance relationships, emails, texting, or don't introduce you to their friends and family.

7. They are elusive, sneaky, frequently working or tired, and may disappear for periods.

8. They are seductive with you but make empty promises — their behavior and words don't match.

9. They're narcissistic, only consider themselves, not your needs.

10. They throw you emotional crumbs or enticing hints of their potential to be loving, then withdraw.

While some of these signs are obvious, others aren't so obvious because sometimes people send mixed messages. An example of this dilemma is a person who may be separated, still legally married or still in quasi-relationship with their ex while simultaneously presenting themselves as single. They may share themselves with you on various levels yet still be unavailable emotionally when it comes down to true transparency, closeness and intimacy. As a narcissist who's emotionally unavailable, they're comfortable dealing with people at a distance while simultaneously expecting them to be close to them; they desire a commitment from others that they're unwilling or sometimes unable to reciprocate. Sometimes this intimacy dilemma can become a tumultuous relationship similar to fighting Mike Tyson in a phone booth; where every time you get close, you get hurt.

Aside from recognizing these obvious signs and mixed signals, the biggest challenge for us is accepting what we see and not rationalizing these signs and signals away. Our willingness and ability to see things for what they are, not what they appear to be or what we want them to be, is the key factor in us not losing time waiting for unrequited love. Whether a person is dealing with emotional unavailability temporarily or it's chronic, it's still time we're investing that we have no way of knowing if it will ever be reciprocated. Some people are simply unwilling or unable to give of themselves in a relationship and need help to get to the place to do so. We may be one of those people and it requires an honest self assessment, willingness and ability to seek that help. Even with that help, there's no way of knowing if this person, or we, may ever be emotionally available. It's the first true commitment they, or we, must make in regards to addressing this commitment phobia; a commitment to self development. And it is through this commitment to self that we learn to develop the trust, honesty, courage and other qualities that are necessary to commit to others who are deserving of us. It's a risk. It's vulnerable. It's frightening at times to depend upon someone to do the right thing with our heart, but it's ultimately worth it when we've found the right person.

www.ingramcontent.com/pod-product-compliance
Lightning Source LLC
Chambersburg PA
CBHW071344280526
45787CB00001B/217